AN
Impartial Account

OF THE LATE

EXPEDITION

AGAINST

ST. AUGUSTINE

UNDER

General *Oglethorpe*.

A FACSIMILE REPRODUCTION
OF THE 1742 EDITION, WITH AN
INTRODUCTION AND INDEXES
BY *Aileen Moore Topping*.

BICENTENNIAL FLORIDIANA
FACSIMILE SERIES.

A University of Florida Book.

University Presses of Florida.
Gainesville 1978.

THE BICENTENNIAL FLORIDIANA
FACSIMILE SERIES
published under the sponsorship of the
BICENTENNIAL COMMISSION
OF FLORIDA,
SAMUEL PROCTOR, *General Editor.*

A FACSIMILE REPRODUCTION
OF THE 1742 EDITION
WITH PREFATORY MATERIAL, INTRODUCTION,
AND INDEXES ADDED.

Library of Congress Cataloging in Publication Data
Main entry under title:

An Impartial account of the late expedition against
 St. Augustine under General Oglethorpe.

 (Bicentennial Floridiana facsimile series)
 Includes bibliographical references.
 1. St. Augustine Expedition, 1740. 2. Oglethorpe, James
Edward, 1696–1785. I. Topping, Aileen Moore. II. Series.
F314.I34 1978   973.2'6   78–21956
ISBN 0–8130–0420–9

BICENTENNIAL COMMISSION OF FLORIDA.

Governor Reubin O'D. Askew, *Honorary Chairman*
Lieutenant Governor J. H. Williams, *Chairman*
Harold W. Stayman, Jr., *Vice Chairman*
William R. Adams, *Executive Director*

Dick J. Batchelor, Orlando
Johnnie Ruth Clarke, St. Petersburg
A. H. "Gus" Craig, St. Augustine
James J. Gardener, Fort Lauderdale
Jim Glisson, Tavares
Mattox Hair, Jacksonville
Thomas L. Hazouri, Jacksonville
Ney C. Landrum, Tallahassee
Mrs. Raymond Mason, Jacksonville
Carl C. Mertins, Jr., Pensacola
Charles E. Perry, Miami
W. E. Potter, Orlando
F. Blair Reeves, Gainesville
Richard R. Renick, Coral Gables
Jane W. Robinson, Cocoa
Mrs. Robert L. Shevin, Tallahassee
Don Shoemaker, Miami
Mary L. Singleton, Jacksonville
Bruce A. Smathers, Tallahassee
Alan Trask, Fort Meade
Edward J. Trombetta, Tallahassee
Ralph D. Turlington, Tallahassee
William S. Turnbull, Orlando
Robert Williams, Tallahassee
Lori Wilson, Merritt Island

THE war of words, threats, and ultimatums between Spain and England which finally erupted into bloody conflict in 1739 was fought not only on the great battlefields of Europe but also in the pine forests and the swamps and along the salt marshes and on the white sand beaches of South Georgia and Northeast Florida. Spain's *la Florida* had once extended from the Keys north to the Chesapeake Bay. The explorations and discoveries of the sixteenth-century conquistadores provided the basis for Spain's claim to this vast territory. Then in 1607 England threw down a daring gauntlet when a group of her colonists under the leadership of Captain John Smith established a settlement at Jamestown. England claimed this territory as her own and named it Virginia in honor of her queen. Spain postured and threatened, but took no decisive action, and the die was cast. Her royal banners began their slow but inexorable retreat southward. In 1629 Charles I granted part of what is now North Carolina to Sir Robert Heath, and Charles II named the area in 1663. Charleston was settled soon after, and in

1733 James Edward Oglethorpe arrived with thirty-five families aboard the galley *Anne* off the Atlantic coast. He selected a townsite on a high bluff overlooking the Savannah River, increasing the threat to the Spanish in St. Augustine and along the St. Johns River. The situation became even more perilous when a settlement was established at Darien, Georgia, to guard the mouth of the Altamaha River, and a number of forts and outposts were erected along the coast. Frederica on St. Simons Island was to become the main bastion on the water route leading from St. Augustine to Savannah. Then there were Fort St. Andrews on Cumberland Island and Fort St. George at the mouth of the St. Johns River itself, just a few miles from the gates of St. Augustine.

It did not matter to Oglethorpe that these fortifications were not on Georgia soil, and Spain's anxieties multiplied. Tension was building, and the relationship between England and Spain was becoming more tenuous, more dangerous with each passing incident. Spain's power was declining, but she was still a force to be reckoned with, and this threat to her Florida borderlands would have to be met. The English forts along the Georgia coast were undermanned and undergunned; they could not resist a Spanish attack. Oglethorpe returned to England in the fall of 1736 to raise a regiment. He was named general of all the British military forces in South Carolina and Georgia, and he was given 600 men, some of whom were stationed on Cumberland Island.

Robert Jenkins, an English seaman and smuggler, was responsible for the name of the conflict, the War of Jenkins' Ear, which began in 1739 between Britain and Spain. The year before, Jenkins had displayed his ear to the members of Parliament, claiming that it had been cut off by his Spanish captors. England's good citizens were outraged at this shameless atrocity and demanded vengeance against the Spanish barbarians. Actually the war was the outgrowth of bitter commercial rivalry, a contest for world dominion, for command of the seas, and for international trade. Oglethorpe had seen it coming for some time and had sought desperately for an alliance with the Creek Indians. In the summer of 1739 he made the long journey to their town, Coweta, on the Chattahoochee River, and secured the pledge of a thousand warriors. Afterwards, Oglethorpe begged South Carolina for money, men, and supplies, but for many reasons, including a dislike of the petitioner, the South Carolinians were slow to respond. The South Carolina General Assembly finally authorized 600 men to come south on a four-month enlistment.

Supported by some 900 regulars and militia, and nearly 1,000 Indians, Oglethorpe moved against Florida in the late spring of 1740. His long siege of St. Augustine failed. The ill-fated expedition further inflamed the enmity which Georgians and Carolinians held for each other, and there were innumerable charges and countercharges. Oglethorpe held that if Charleston support had come earlier, his venture would have been successful. Citizens of Charleston and the South Carolina General Assembly argued otherwise, and they prepared a report which set forth the degree of their support of Oglethorpe. When this document was suppressed for political reasons, it generated still another report, *An Impartial Account of the Late Expedition against St. Augustine under General Oglethorpe*, which was published in 1742. It is this important document, long out of print, that Aileen Moore Topping has edited for publication in the Bicentennial Floridiana Facsimile Series. Although the *Impartial Account* was published anonymously in London in 1742, Mrs. Topping's painstaking research shows that its author was James Killpatrick, a former resident of Charleston, who also paid the printing bill. This volume complements the *Relation, or Journal, of a Late Expedition to the Gates of St. Augustine, on Florida* which was earlier edited for publication by John Jay TePaske for the same series, published by University Presses of Florida for the American Revolution Bicentennial Commission of Florida.

Aileen Moore Topping is a graduate of Agnes Scott College and Middlebury College and has taught at the University of Miami. She has worked extensively in the Spanish archives at the Archivo General de Simancas, the Archivo Historico Nacional, and the Archivo General de Indias. Mrs. Topping is continuing her research and writing of Florida colonial history at her residence in Orange Park, Florida.

SAMUEL PROCTOR.
General Editor of the
BICENTENNIAL FLORIDIANA
FACSIMILE SERIES.

Introduction.

THROUGHOUT the year 1737 reports reached London of an expeditionary force being prepared in Havana for a descent upon Georgia to expel that new colony from Spanish territory. Those reports had important effects. For several years the British Crown had ignored Spanish protests against the encroachment on Florida by English colonists and Spanish demands that the territorial boundary between Florida and the English colonies be fixed. In September 1737 the government of Prime Minister Robert Walpole answered the latest demand by proposing that the question of boundaries and other disputes which had arisen between the two nations be settled in a conference of commissioners to be named by the two sovereigns.

Thomás Geraldino, Spanish minister plenipotentiary, was no match for the Duke of Newcastle, British foreign secretary. Geraldino was later reprimanded for having accepted on behalf of his Court the proposal conveyed to him, without at the same time insisting upon certain conditions stipulated by his sovereign—that the forts built in Spanish territory by Mr. James Edward Oglethorpe be demolished, that the disputed territory be evacuated, and that the conference of commissioners be limited to a period of not more than six months.[1]

King Philip V immediately canceled the expedition against Georgia. Although his order to that effect was issued on 28 November 1737, it was not received in Havana until 21 March 1738, a few hours before the main body of the expeditionary force was to set sail.[2] Commissioners met at El Pardo in January 1739, only to suspend their deliberations in October of that year when England declared war on Spain. The conflict was called the War of Jenkins' Ear, because in 1738 Captain Robert Jenkins, a British seaman, exhibited to the House of Commons his ear, which he said had been slit off seven years earlier by a Spanish *guardacostas* captain who had arrested him for smuggling in the West Indies.

Another effect of the rumors of imminent danger to Georgia was an increase in the influence of the twenty-four members of Parliament who were Trustees of Georgia. Together with powerful mercantile interests, they were able to contravene Walpole's pacific policy toward Spain. In a meeting of the Privy Council on 24 April 1737, the Georgia Trustees were denied permission to form an infantry regiment with the command and a commission as colonel to be given to Oglethorpe.

That decision was soon reversed, so that when Oglethorpe returned to Georgia it was as a major general with a regiment of 700 men and the command of British forces in South Carolina and Georgia.

During Oglethorpe's previous sojourns in America, from January 1733 to May 1734 and from February to November 1736, he had built a line of forts southward: Forts Frederica and St. Simons on St. Simons Island, Forts William and St. Andrews on Cumberland Island, and Fort St. George on the north shore at the mouth of the St. Johns River. The Trustees for the Establishment of the Colony of Georgia had been authorized on 9 June 1732 to settle the territory between the Savannah and Altamaha rivers. Only the two forts on St. Simons Island were within the Georgia grant. All of the forts were on islands which for more than a century had been the sites of flourishing Spanish missions until, in the last years of the seventeenth century and the first of the eighteenth, the depredations of hostile Indians, corsairs, and Carolina traders forced the governors of St. Augustine to withdraw the missions from Guale.

Oglethorpe's fort at the mouth of the St. Johns was intolerable to Spain. In July 1736 Juan Francisco de Güemes y Horcasitas, governor of Havana, sent the engineer Antonio de Arredondo to convey to Oglethorpe a demand that Fort St. George be demolished. Arredondo also had orders to examine the colony of Georgia and to determine what reinforcements and new fortifications were needed in Florida. Güemes sent Oglethorpe copies of Article VII of the Treaty of Madrid, which in 1670 recognized England's possession of lands in America which she held at that time, and of Article VIII of the Anglo-Spanish treaty, which was part of the Peace of Utrecht in 1713. In the Treaty of Utretcht, Queen Anne of Great Britain promised to aid the Spaniards in order that the former boundaries of their dominions in America be restored and established as they were in the time of the Spanish king Charles II (1661–1700), if it were found that they had suffered any infraction after his death. Güemes asked that English encroachment on Spanish lands be stopped and that usurped territory be evacuated.

In reply, Oglethorpe cited King Charles II's charter to the Lords Proprietors of Carolina, which in 1665 granted to them territory southward to 29 degrees of latitude, and included St. Augustine, then one hundred years old. Oglethorpe insisted that he had not enlarged the dominions of his sovereign but had only regulated them, and that without further orders he could not change his policy. He agreed to demolish Fort St. George, but said that the question of boundaries could be settled only by the two Crowns.[3] Later Oglethorpe sent his aide, Charles Dempsey, to St. Augustine. Dempsey was able to arrange on

18 October 1736 a so-called treaty with the governor of Florida, Francisco del Moral Sánchez Villegas, which temporarily accepted the status quo. Güemes considered the "treaty" a breach of faith on the part of Oglethorpe and a ploy designed only to gain time. The Spanish king immediately declared the agreement void because neither party had authority to make a treaty, and Moral Sánchez was removed from office forthwith.[4]

Colonel Manuel de Montiano, late of the infantry of Aragón, was appointed governor of Florida by the same royal cédula of 12 April 1737 which dismissed Moral Sánchez.[5] From the time of his arrival at St. Augustine, Montiano sought intelligence about the English colonies to the north. In July 1738 he sent Juan Ignazio de los Reyes, an astute Iguaja Indian who lived at Pocotalaca near St. Augustine, to reconnoiter the Georgia coast. The scout went in a small canoe from Picolata to Cumberland Island, where he asked for asylum, saying that he had killed another Indian in St. Augustine and was fleeing from Spanish authorities. He was taken to Fort St. Andrews and then to St. Simons, where the commanding officer, Lieutenant Colonel Cochran, asked him many questions about the Spanish expedition which had been canceled in March of that year, and about the defenses of St. Augustine. Cochran wanted to know if the castillo could be mined, if there was water inside the fort, if there was much money in the town, and so on, saying that soon all would belong to the king of Great Britain.

Cochran had just returned from England. He told the Indian scout that as soon as General Oglethorpe arrived with his 700 men, they and the 900 divided between St. Simons, St. Andrews, and Savannah and the 5,000 to 6,000 Indians who could be called up within two months would lay siege to St. Augustine. They would begin the operation by capturing a small fort on the St. Johns River seven leagues from the presidio. Cochran said that the soldiers then in Georgia had been brought there to capture St. Augustine, but when news of the Spanish expeditionary force in Havana reached Georgia, Oglethorpe changed his plan and went to England to procure more men. The Indian's report was corroborated by sworn depositions taken from three deserters from St. Simons, who had come to the village of Nombre de Dios de Atacaris.

At about the same time the quartermaster, Captain Sebastián Sánchez, went up the coast as far as Port Royal with 16 men in a piragua in search of 8 forced laborers who had escaped from a lime kiln where they were working. He reported to Montiano that he had seen no new fortifications on the coast but that there were many soldiers in Georgia. At Frederica he was told that 400 soldiers and 200 laborers had just arrived there.[6]

Meanwhile Governor Güemes had sent to St. Augustine the 8 pickets of 50 men each who had come from Spain to Havana for the Georgia expedition, and with them 12 cannon. He had also sent from Havana the engineers Arredondo and Ruiz de Olano, a master mason, a master ironworker, 2 carpenters, 6 stonecutters, and 82 forced laborers to improve the fortifications at St. Augustine and Apalache.[7]

Early in 1739 Captain Pedro Lamberto went from Florida to Charleston, ostensibly to consult a physician. There he learned that there was friction between Oglethorpe and the South Carolinians, who refused to recognize him as their commander-in-chief.[8] In July of that year Juan Castelnau, assistant paymaster at Pensacola, gave information about Georgia to the governor of Havana. While traveling with permission from St. Augustine to Charleston, Castelnau had been arrested in Georgia. During the eighteen months that he spent in prison there, he learned that in July 1738 Colonel Cochran had brought to St. Simons 300 men whom he had taken out of Gibraltar, and that two months later Oglethorpe had arrived with three transports, one warship, and a packet, all loaded with men and munitions. Castelnau had heard officers of General Oglethorpe's regiment say that they had come to America to take St. Augustine.[9]

Throughout 1739 Oglethorpe reinforced his garrisons with militia and Indians who were sent with increasing frequency on border raids into Florida. In March, when a committee from the South Carolina General Assembly stopped at St. Simons en route to St. Augustine to demand the return of runaway slaves, Oglethorpe took advantage of the opportunity to send with them Lieutenant Raymond Deméré "to present his compliments to the governor." Deméré's efforts to obtain intelligence for his superior were frustrated by Montiano's insistence upon entertaining all the Englishmen as his houseguests.[10]

Later that year the general himself traveled to Coweta, deep in the interior of the country, to enlist the assistance of the Creek and Cherokee nations in an attack on St. Augustine. On 5 October he informed the Trustees of Georgia that he had sent Toonahowi against the Spaniards with 200 men. Toonahowi was one of the Indians who had been entertained by the Trustees in London when he was taken there by Oglethorpe in 1734. Oglethorpe told the Trustees that the Cherokees were raising 600 men and the Creeks 400, "who will act with me."[11]

On 27 September 1739 Oglethorpe informed Lieutenant Governor William Bull of South Carolina that he had orders "to annoy the Subjects of the King of Spain." He asked that the province of South Carolina join him in an expedition against

St. Augustine, warning, "If we do not attack, we shall be attacked."[12] South Carolina had no reason to fear an attack from Florida. In a letter dated 27 March 1738, the day before the scheduled launching of the expedition against Georgia, Governor Güemes had assured the governor of South Carolina, quoting the pertinent articles of the treaties of Madrid and Utrecht, that the operation was to be directed only against usurped territory, not against lands legally held by Great Britain as was the case with Carolina.[13]

But the people of South Carolina had another reason to desire the destruction of St. Augustine. Since 1727 there had been in effect in Florida royal orders which protected fugitive Negro slaves. The provisions of those orders were changed several times. At first the royal officials of St. Augustine were authorized to pay the owners for fugitive slaves who had been converted to the Roman Catholic faith, and the slaves became the property of the Crown. By a royal cédula of 22 October 1733, Philip V granted freedom to runaway slaves who adopted the Catholic faith and served a term of four years of labor for the state. Later this labor requirement was removed. St. Augustine was particularly attractive to Negroes who had been brought to South Carolina from Portuguese Angola, where they had learned something of the Portuguese language and of the Roman church. The slaves who were responsible for several deaths in an insurrection at Stono in South Carolina in September 1739 were identified by General Oglethorpe as natives of Angola.[14] Spanish agents and missionary priests were accused of inciting them to rebellion and desertion.

Eager as they may have been to destroy St. Augustine, the members of the South Carolina General Assembly were obliged to consider very carefully the question of joining Oglethorpe in the enterprise he proposed. Funds in the provincial treasury were low, Charleston had suffered an epidemic of smallpox, and the danger of insurrection made it unwise to send many men away from the province. After studying the matter, the Commons House resolved on 12 December, the council concurring, "In case General Oglethorpe should think it proper to form a Design of besieging St. Augustine and should communicate his Scheme to the General Assembly, and should make it appear that the same was probable of being attended with the Success of taking or demolishing that Garrison, that then the Public of this Province would engage to give General Oglethorpe the best Assistance they reasonably could to put his Scheme into Execution."

Oglethorpe's reply, dated 29 December 1739 and received on 30 January 1740, contained a list of the things he thought reasonable and necessary for South Carolina to provide. He did not mention the number of men to be supplied by the province. The general promised to "spare no personal Labour or Danger towards freeing Carolina of a Place from whence their Negroes were encouraged to massacre their Masters, and were openly harboured after such Attempts." Because two men had been killed on Amelia Island by Yamasee Indians who were allies of the Spaniards, Oglethorpe had already made a raid into Florida.

On 4 February the assembly received two letters from Oglethorpe, written on 23 January. He reported that a detachment of British soldiers and Indians had captured the two small Spanish forts called Picolata and San Francisco de Pupo, on opposite shores of the St. Johns River, and he sent a list of the assistance he would require for an expedition against St. Augustine. The assembly decided that the province could not afford the estimated cost of the supplies, 209,492 pounds, 10 shillings (Carolina currency), but that, "If the General would certify . . . that the same [expedition] was probable of being attended with the Success of taking that Garrison with an assistance from this Government of an Expence amounting to the sum of 120,000 pounds . . . that then the Publick of this Province would be willing to be at that Expence." General Oglethorpe replied with the promise that he would come to Charleston.

In Charleston on 26 March, Oglethorpe wrote to Bull: "It would be best immediately to make a sudden Attempt which might be done with an

Expence of only Part of the Sum intended. If this Attempt could not be immediately made, that the only Measure would be the giving him at present such Part of the Assistance proposed as might keep the War on the other Side of St. John's or St. Mattheo's River until the Fall, during which Time Preparations might be made for the Siege at an Expence within the Sum voted by the Assembly." He added that if neither course could be followed, the two provinces must prepare to defend themselves, and that the Spaniards would regain control of the St. Johns River and the lines of communication with Apalache and the French at Mobile.

When the Commons House asked for an estimate of what would be needed for a sudden attempt, Oglethorpe gave a list of the men and matériel he would expect. He added, "If these Preparations could not be made within fourteen Days so as to set out from Charlestown within that Time, the Enterprize would hardly succeed." Having found that the supplies could not be ready that quickly, the house wanted to know from the general, "What Supplies he thought necessary to keep the War on the other Side of St. John's River." Oglethorpe then offered to wait longer for supplies in order to make the sudden attempt that he preferred.

In a conference with members of both houses, Oglethorpe assured them that he did not doubt his being able to capture St. Augustine quickly.

Aware of the longstanding enmity between the Carolina traders and the French at Mobile, he warned that "in Case the Havanna was taken, the Spaniards would in all Probability, rather call in the French to Augustine, than let it fall into our Hands." Captain Vincent Pearse, commodore of British naval forces in the area, who was present at the conference, promised that "he would answer for it the Place would have no relief by Sea, and that they all ought to be hanged if they did not take it in a very short time." On 5 April both houses accepted the general's plan, and preparations for the expedition were begun immediately.[15]

It appears that misunderstandings as to the purpose of the enterprise, the plan of campaign, the conduct of operations, and the division of authority and command existed from the inception of the undertaking. When the expedition failed, recriminations were inevitable. Members of the South Carolina General Assembly and the local citizens were incensed to learn that Oglethorpe had claimed that the contributions of South Carolina were tardy and insufficient and that certain Carolina officers were guilty of insubordination, among them the experienced Indian fighter Colonel John Palmer and Colonel Alexander Vanderdussen, commanding officer of the South Carolina regiment.

On 18 July, two weeks after Oglethorpe had ordered withdrawal of the expeditionary forces from Florida, the Commons House resolved "That a Representation should be immediately prepared, and laid before His Majesty, in which should be set forth, in a particular Manner, what Measures have been taken lately by this Province for the Reduction of St. Augustine, in which we have exerted ourselves to the Utmost, and brought a greater Debt on the Public than our present Circumstances are well able to bear."

The house appointed Attorney General James Abercromby, Captain Robert Austin, Colonel Robert Brewton, John Dart, Thomas Drayton, William Elliot, Captain Henry Hyrne, Isaac Mazyck, Captain Samuel Morris, Jacob Motte, and Major William Pinckney as a committee "to enquire into the Causes of the Disappointment of Success in the late Expedition against St. Augustine under the Command of General Oglethorpe." That committee conscientiously based its findings solely upon "Extracts of Journals . . . Examinations on Oath, and original Letters." The report submitted almost one year after the appointment of the committee was accompanied by an appendix of 139 corroborating documents. After considering the "principal and most apparent Causes of the ill Success that attended this most extraordinary Expedition," the committee had found that "neither the General nor the Commodore have taken any proper or vigorous Steps toward the Reduction of St. Augustine or done what they engaged to do, and therefore they are of Opinion that this Government hath been greatly misled by both."

After approving the report, the General Assembly engaged the local printer Peter Timothy to publish it. Some three months later, impatient with the slow progress of the printer, the assembly sent the documents to Peregrine Fury, London agent of the province, with orders to have both report and appendix published in England. By that time the bitter dispute between General Oglethorpe and South Carolina had spread to London, where both adversaries had their advocates. More delay ensued.

James Glen, the newly appointed governor of South Carolina, had not yet left England for America. Peregrine Fury turned to Glen for guidance and when he found that in Glen's opinion the report was "not calculated for the meridian of London," Fury further delayed the printing. On 18 May 1742 Lieutenant Governor Bull sent the commons a letter dated 29 January from Fury in which the agent promised that "His Excellency Governor Glen would acquaint the Committee with the particular Reasons that had prevailed with the Agent to desist from printing and publishing the Report of the Committee appointed to enquire into the Causes of the Disappointment of Success in the late Expedition against St. Augustine, etc."

The Commons House immediately ordered the documents to be printed in Charleston and appointed a committee "to enquire into the Reasons given by Mr. Fury . . . and [his] conduct . . . in the Dispute between this Province and the Colony of Georgia." On 1 June 1742 the house was told, "Your Committee are apprehensive that our Agent has private Reasons to dissuade him from publishing any printed Papers, wherein the least Imputation of Blame can any way be laid on General Oglethorpe, who, your Committee are informed, employs Mr. Fury as Agent for his Regiment of Foot at Georgia." Consideration of the committee's report was postponed, and it was not until May 1744 that the house reprimanded the agent for ignoring its instructions.[16]

The surgeon James Killpatrick, a former resident of Charleston, was living in London in the summer of 1742. Little is known of Killpatrick's early life; it has been conjectured that he was educated at Edinburgh, as a student of that name was enrolled there in 1708–9. Killpatrick made an ocean crossing in 1717 or 1718, which may have been his emigration to America. In South Carolina his name appears in the will books: in 1724, as executor of the will of David Kilpatrick [sic]; in 1727, as executor of the will of Thomas Hepworth, secretary of the province and Killpatrick's father-in-law; in 1732, in the will of Thomas Cooper, Gentleman, who bequeathed to him a gift of Greek, Latin, and English books; and in 1734, in the will of Benjamin Godfrey, Berkeley County planter, which mentions a parcel of land sold to Dr. David Kilpatrick [*sic*], executors to convey said land to James Kilpatrick [*sic*], son of said David Kilpatrick [*sic*]. His purchases and sales of land are recorded in Charleston. His name is mentioned in the *South Carolina Gazette* several times after 1734 in connection with the practice of medicine.

The death of Killpatrick's son Thomas in the smallpox epidemic of 1738 may have caused him to persist in the use of inoculation against the disease in spite of widespread criticism. The practice of inoculation was denounced by the *South Carolina Gazette* and by Dr. Thomas Dale, a prominent physician, and was finally prohibited by the General Assembly. In 1739 Killpatrick published in Charleston a pamphlet, *A Full and Clear Reply to Doctor T. Dale*, which he later developed into a longer paper, *The Analysis of Inoculation*, published in London in 1754, and later translated into several European languages. Having changed his name and acquired the degree, he signed the name Dr. J. Kirkpatrick to the essays, translations, and Latin and English poetry he published from 1749 to 1772.[17]

It is thought that Killpatrick was established in London by July 1742, several weeks after the assembly had received the letter in which Fury gave his reasons for not publishing the report of the committee "appointed to enquire into the Causes of the Disappointment of Success in the late Expedition against St. Augustine under the Command of General Oglethorpe." In a letter dated 7 September 1742 the South Carolina Committee of Correspondence instructed Fury to deliver the copy of the report which was in his possession to Colonel Alexander Vanderdussen who was going to London, "in order to make what Use of it he should find in his Power for the Service of this Province." Whether Killpatrick first read the report and the appendix in Charleston or in London, he certainly had access to a copy of the report when he took it upon himself to write and publish a faithful abstract of it. Killpatrick did not prepare an abstract of the appendix, which was at that time "in the Hands of their Agent, Mr. Fury," but in his preface he wrote, "No Proof or Paper is cited in this, of which the Relator has not, by the Favour of Friends, seen the Original, or authentic Copies."

Killpatrick's *Impartial Account . . . Occasioned by The Suppression of the Report, made by a Committee of the General Assembly in South-Carolina* was published anonymously and at the author's expense. It is a skillful précis of the report which omits no important circumstance, and it is the work of an accomplished polemicist. The few discrepancies either are minor or are readily discernible, as for example the substitution of the name "Pupa" for "Picolata" on page 32 of the *Impartial Account*. Where new facts are introduced, the *Impartial Account* makes more vivid the sense of the report. An example of this intensification of meaning is the paragraph on pages 27–28 concerning General Oglethorpe's offer to show his orders to Colonel Vanderdussen and "another Gentleman then present," after the colonel had expressed his "great Dissatisfaction at this mortifying Retreat," when Oglethorpe said that "he had done all that was expected from his Orders . . . intimating that the Design was only to draw the *Spaniards* Attention from *Cuba*."

Killpatrick regretted that the two gentlemen had not examined those orders, and he suggested that perusal of them was still desirable. It was unreasonable to think that they were the orders of 15 June 1739 "to annoy" the Spaniards and that Oglethorpe had received no further directions, particularly after the declaration of war. Killpatrick suggested that from the beginning Oglethorpe had not taken the government and the officers of South Carolina into his confidence, "Nor indeed can it be supposed at all improbable from the whole Conduct of this Affair, that it was influenced by such Orders [to draw attention from Cuba]. . . . And if this Siege were in Truth but a Feint, might not that have been effected without such an Expence . . . ?"

Killpatrick's *Impartial Account* was attacked by George Cadogan, a lieutenant in Oglethorpe's regiment, in a pamphlet entitled *The Spanish Hireling Detected: Being a Refutation of the Several Calumnies and Falsehoods in a late Pamphlet,* etc. (London, 1743). Still writing anonymously, in *A Full Reply to Lieut. Cadogan's Spanish Hireling,* etc. (London, 1743), and in articles published in the *Champion* and the *London Magazine,* Killpatrick answered Cadogan and other critics.[18]

General Oglethorpe gave his explanation for the failure of the expedition in a letter to William Bull: "Sir, To satisfy our Friends, though I have but little Time, I shall trouble you with a long Letter which I believe will clear up all Objections concerning the Management of the present Expedition. Augustine cannot be closely shut up without dividing the Troops that besiege it. There must be one Party on the Main, one on St. Anastatia, and one on Quartell; which I could not do until the Seas spared the 200 from the Island. You must remember that I mentioned that Augustine was scarce of Food, the Entrenchment around the Town weak, and the Garrison not compleated. I therefore insisted to attack it immediately since all Hope of Success lay in Speed, and that, as I apprehended, if we delayed, Succours would come from Cuba. . . . After I left Charles Town and before the Troops got to the Rendezvous, six Half Galleys with long brass Nine-Pounders got into Augustine with two Sloops loaded with Provisions. . . . It was impossible to carry heavy Cannon, and mount them, and make Trenches without Pioneers. And you know when I proposed 400 of them, Whites or Negroes, it was an Expence the Province could not afford. . . . The Commodore and the Sea Officers agreed with me that they would attack the Galleys, which, if taken, was to be followed by Colonel Vander Dussen attacking the Town on the Water-side at the same Time as I was to attack it on the Land. I accordingly went on the Main. . . . The Commodore acquainted me that the Council of War found it impracticable to attack the Half Galleys, and that they were obliged to leave the Coast on the 5th Day of July, and that several Vessels loaded with Provisions were got into the Metanzas for the Spaniards. . . . With respect to the Affair at Moosa . . . the Occasion of losing that Party was the disobeying my Orders."[19]

In Spanish accounts Oglethorpe's attempt to capture St. Augustine is called a siege. One report was written by Captain Domingo de la Cruz, naval commandant and chief pilot of St. Augustine, who in May 1740 was captured by an English war frigate when he went out from the presidio bound for Guarico, carrying 6,000 pesos with which to buy food for the garrison of St. Augustine. The Spanish money was confiscated, and captain and crew were taken to Charleston as prisoners. Cruz was released on 13 August with license to take ship for England. He disembarked at Bayonne and went overland to Madrid, where on 9 October he presented to the king a journal of what he had observed in South Carolina. He began his report with the departure from Charleston on 25 May of six 20-gun frigates and two packets with 1,400 men, and concluded it with the return of the Carolinians on 2 August. "Because this enterprise did not have the effect they had confidently expected, the whole province has been thrown into a state of great consternation. After six days of meetings they have decided to represent to their king the great effort they had made for the conquest of St. Augustine . . . and to beg for assistance so that they can again lay siege to that plaza."[20]

The engineer Pedro Ruiz de Olano sent to the king on 8 August a report of the siege in which he said that in twenty-seven days of continuous fire only the parapets of the castillo had been damaged badly, recommending that they be made thicker at once, because it was logical that if General Oglethorpe again lay siege to St. Augustine, he would place his batteries on the mainland to give him more effective firepower.[21]

Franciscan Fray Francisco de San Buenaventura y Tejada, auxiliary bishop of Santiago de Cuba, was in St. Augustine at the time of the siege. After the departure of the English, he sent a day-by-day account of the ordeal to Dr. Joseph Ortigoza of Seville, Spain, who had the letter published in that city. The bishop stated that when the attack began, the people of St. Augustine took as their protector the Most Holy Mary of the Rosary and decided that at every shot, whether fired by the enemy or by the defenders, no sound should be heard in the city except the Hail Mary. He claimed that the miraculous protection enjoyed by the people was demonstrated in several ways: the camp at Moze was recovered with minimal losses, valuable information about the English encampment was given by a deserter who came into the plaza, cannonballs fired from Anastasia Island by the enemy fell harmlessly into the bay, and although the convoy of provisions which came from Havana was observed by the enemy, he made no effort to capture it, which could have been done with ease.[22]

Governor Montiano reported to Havana and Madrid in a series of letters. As early as November 1739 he feared that a siege was imminent, because the previous month a 24-gun English frigate had captured an advice boat that he had dispatched for Havana. Later the same frigate had been sighted off Matanzas Inlet. Montiano urgently requested that provisions be sent from Cuba and Mexico, because the English merchants of New York who had been purveying food to the presidio would undoubtedly be ordered to stop their shipments to Florida. Work on the castillo, he noted, was progressing, but it still lacked a covered way which could serve as a refuge for the civilians of the town.[23]

On 31 January 1740 Montiano reported that in the previous month two outriders of Captain Lamberto's dragoons had been killed while returning from Apalache, the garrison at Picolata had repulsed an attack led by a British officer, and parties of white men and Indians had been sighted in the grasslands south of the St. Johns River. He had decided to reinforce the small fort on Diego de Espinosa's ranch and had sent men out to round up cattle and move them to Santa Anastasia Island and to bring horses into the plaza. On 18 January, Juan Ignazio de los Reyes had reported seeing 12 vessels and about 700 men at San Nicolás, and on 21 January he had brought news that Fort Picolata had been burned to the ground and Fort Francisco de Pupo captured. Diego de Espinosa and six soldiers had been sent to examine all harbors near the mouth of the St. Johns; at San Nicolás they saw three campaign tents on the north shore.

Montiano described the great river as "an arm of the sea three-quarters of a league wide." Without naval power, he pointed out, he could do absolutely nothing: the English had control of the St. Johns River; they had vessels large enough to transport artillery of moderate size; and they could be reinforced at any time by way of the channels which stretched from port to port as far north as Port Royal. No attempt against them without sea power would be effective.[24]

Montiano informed Güemes on 23 February that on the St. Johns was a place called Mojoloa where the channel was very close to the shore; there all boats attempting to go south to Pupo would be exposed to gunfire. He had decided to build a small fort there with six or seven 8-pound guns and 50 men under a captain. To enable him to do that, he required three or four of the galliots which had been built in the Havana shipyards for the aborted 1738 expedition. He hoped that with the galliots he could recover Pupo and re-establish communication with Apalache. Later Ruiz de Olano and Pedro Lamberto chose the narrows at San Nicolás as a more advantageous place, but the scarcity of food at St. Augustine was so extreme that Montiano had to abandon the idea of sending a detachment to build and man a fort there.[25]

On 25 March, Montiano dispatched to Havana a list of the men he had available for the defense of the presidio: 462 soldiers, 61 militia, 50 Indians, and 40 free Negroes.[26] On 27 April he reported the safe arrival on 14 April of 6 galliots with a complement of 122 men under the command of Captain Juan de León Fandino and Captain Francisco del Castillo, and of two launches laden with food and ammunition brought from Havana by Captain Domingo de la Cruz.[27]

By late June, Montiano had reported that the port was blockaded, although Matanzas Inlet was still open, and that the English had occupied Fort San Diego, Santa Anastasia Island, the settlement of Gracia Real (also called Moze), and San Matheo Point. Families of the town had taken refuge under the protection of the guns of the fort. Despite the gravity of the situation, Montiano wrote, "Nothing causes me anxiety except the want of provisions . . . if we get no more supplies we shall die of hunger."[28]

When Montiano reported that he had recovered the camp at Moze, he sent the king a paper found earlier near there: "To whom it may concern, greetings: You are informed that as the King of Great Britain has declared war on Philip of Borbón, King of Spain, because of cruelties committed against English traders, . . . and because many Spanish subjects, especially Catalonians, have given reason to believe that they will not obey a bad government if their ancient privileges are not restored, if there is any Catalonian, or other Spaniard, Indian, or Negro, who wishes to pass from the garrison of St. Augustine to this camp, the Spaniard will be treated as such, the Negro or Indian will be freed. . . . And if they wish to join us they will be accepted."[29]

Montiano's report to the king dated 9 August was a review of the siege:

> Sire: I bring to Your Majesty's attention that several English frigates and other vessels of different classes having stood offshore before this port from 31 March until a few days ago, it happened that on 13 June this plaza was besieged by the generals James Oglethorpe, commandant of the land forces, and Vincent Pierse [*sic*], commodore of the maritime forces. The former brought 500 men and many banners to the village of Gracia Real where I had placed the free Negroes, 300 men to the shore at San Matheo, and an equal number to the island of Santa Anastasia. The latter came with seven warships of different burdens, one of them a 50-gun ship, one with 40 guns, another with 28, and four with 20; three sloops, twelve schooners, twenty-three launches and boats, a few piraguas, and three packets. The besieging force comprised 450 soldiers of General Oglethorpe's regiment, 40 horse, 600 militia from Carolina and Georgia, 130 Indians of various nations, 200 armed sailors encamped on Santa Anastasia Island and 200 who manned the schooners and sloops, and the piraguas which were used to transport food and ammunition from one place to another within the bar.
>
> They set up three batteries against us, one opposite the fort in the place called the Loza on Santa Anastasia Island with four 18-pound

guns and one 9-pounder with which they fired on the galliots; a second on the wooded point of the same island with two 18-pounders; and another on San Matheo Point with seven 6-pounders, five of them made of iron, the others of bronze. In those three batteries they placed four mortars for firing grenades weighing half a hundred-weight and about one hundred-weight, and three small mortars for firing hand grenades and grenades weighing 6, 8, 10, and 12 pounds.

Bombardment and firing from the batteries continued for twenty-seven consecutive days, from 24 June until 20 July, whereupon the besiegers set out in precipitate ignominious flight. They left behind four 6-pound guns, one schooner, several rifles and muskets, a quantity of cannon balls and grenades, two barrels of powder, and some gun carriages for use on sea and land. They set fire to several barrels of meat, cheese and butter, dried meat, rice, and beans, and to a schooner, and a beautiful mortar carriage. Our people salvaged some barrels of flour, butter, rice, biscuits, and bacon. We experienced some damage in the fortress which must be repaired at once. One artilleryman and one convict were killed by cannon balls. One soldier and one Negro slave were wounded by grenades; the latter has recovered completely; the former has a good chance of surviving, but with the loss of one leg.

I must tell Your Majesty without delay that the right hand of the Omnipotent has miraculously inspired in this garrison and civilian population such spirit, zeal, and valor, that besides having persevered tirelessly with weapons in their hands day and night throughout the siege, even the Negro slaves, whom I had also armed with rifles and bayonets, longed to rush out to meet the enemy's attacks.

These ardent Spaniards distinguished themselves on the following occasion. Having been assured by my spies that in the quarters at the village of Gracia Real, also called Moze, there was a detachment of little more than 100 men, I sent out of the plaza at midnight on 25 June a party of about 300 men, dragoons, convicts, Indians, and free Negroes, under the command of Captain Antonio Salgado. Moving slowly and cautiously they were able by two o'clock in the morning to lie in ambush near the camp. At three o'clock the Scots called out the watchword, and our men, who were ready for action, realized that they had already been perceived. They showed themselves all at once, and met a heavy fire from the enemy. Taking advantage of this juncture, they advanced with such impetus that in less than three quarters of an hour, the duration of the skirmish, there surrendered at bayonet point a company of 72 Scots, chosen men who were General Oglethorpe's guards, 15 infantrymen and a sergeant from General Oglethorpe's regiment, 40 horse, and 35 Indians, Yuchis and Uchises.

That detachment or garrison, which was commanded by Colonel Palma [*sic*], the man who in the year '28 dared to approach within the distance of two rifle shots of this fortress to make certain demands of Field Marshal Don Antonio de Benavides, was entirely undone and destroyed. Our men left 75 dead and took out 35 prisoners and their flag, among the prisoners a captain and three subalterns, all Scots; among the dead, Colonel Palma and his son, a cavalry captain. I think that many others went out to die in the thickets of the forests, as afterwards several bodies were found there, and on the river bank we have found the clothing of others who threw themselves into the stream. I have learned of the escape of only 11 Indians and 7 horse who were out on patrol and did not meet our party, perhaps by special providence.

The six galliots with 122 crewmen sent to me by the governor of Havana for the purpose of recovering Pupo have prevented schooners and other smaller vessels from entering the bay which lies before this city. In summary, Sire, I can report to Your Majesty that amid the intense stubborn persistence of the fire of cannon and mortars and the anxiety naturally aroused by the multitude of vessels of every burden which were in our sight, that not only did no Spaniard desert in all the time of the siege, but no one complained, although all these faithful soldiers and subjects were supplied only one pound of bread, half rations for the infantry, and everyone knew that from the 15th day of

July there were rations for no more than another fortnight.

On 27 July there came into this port by way of Matanzas Inlet three sloops and two schooners laden with food sent to me by the governor of Havana, and with casava, corn, rice, and 700-weight of flour sent by the viceroy of New Spain and the governor and royal officials of Vera Cruz. Because of my repeated requests made in view of Your Majesty's royal orders and the needs of this plaza, I expect more succor. Those ships could not come into this port earlier because of the danger posed by the enemy warships which except for a few intervals have stood off this port since 2 October of last year. I received a message from Mosquito Inlet on the night of 7 July that those vessels had put in there on the previous day, but I took no steps toward transporting those provisions for important reasons, especially because of intelligence given me by a deserter that the enemy intended to advance on the city by sea and land with one of the spring tides.

As soon as the spring tides had ended, I sent Ensign Don Antonio Nieto de Carvajal with two launches, one boat, and a piragua to fetch the victuals. On the lee shore of Matanzas Inlet he encountered a frigate and a packet which fired on him persistently and put out two launches and two boats to pursue him. He defended himself bravely, and returned here with almost 800-weight of flour. This method of transporting the food was continued safely until the ships mentioned above could put in here, after the retreat of the enemies and the departure of the frigate and packet which remained on this coast for four days after the siege was lifted.

All the nineteen English deserters who are here have assured me that General Oglethorpe is now at the mouth of the St. Johns River with his troops, militia, and marine forces. They say that at times he states that he intends to attack this plaza again soon, at other times that he will continue the retreat to his colony, and again that he will lay siege to this plaza next spring. Some of the deserters say that he will have 2,000 men for the second siege; others say that he will conduct the operation with 2 regiments which are to come from London. Although I am persuaded that the rebuff he has suffered and his disgraceful flight can afford him nothing but universal disrespect, nonetheless, because of the influence that general can exert over personalities consonant with his restless and captious nature, I humbly beg Your Majesty to send me a reinforcement of men, ordnance, and warlike stores.

In the present war the English have diminished my garrison as follows: in the capture of Pupo, one sergeant, ten soldiers, and one Indian; in the sloop which belonged to this plaza they captured forty-eight men, among them gunners, sailors, and the naval officers of this presidio, and six thousand pesos; at Fort San Diego twenty-four soldiers, two sergeants, nine horse, and three Indians, at the moment when one watch was about to relieve the other; at Matanzas three soldiers who were carrying messages; another courier dispatched to me from Apalache; in the sally to Moze one ensign and eleven soldiers killed, two wounded; two men killed outside the plaza; and in the siege one gunner killed and one soldier wounded. I again assure Your Majesty that in the meantime, until Your Majesty orders to be sent here the assistance which this plaza needs for its defense, I shall defend the plaza diligently as is my duty, even to giving my life in its defense.

The enclosed instruments are word for word copies of a summons from the generals Oglethorpe and Pierse and of the response made to it:

To His Excellency Don Manuel de Montiano, Governor and Captain General of Florida and the garrison of St. Augustine, the Very Illustrious and Very Reverend Bishop and Father in God, the Honourable War Council, officers, soldiers, and citizens of this Plaza: We the undersigned James Oglethorpe, General of the Army of His Britannic Majesty, and Vincent Pierse, Commodore of the warships and naval forces of His Britannic Majesty which at present are before the city of St. Augustine, summon you to surrender to His Most Excellent Majesty George II, King of Great Britain, France, and Ireland, etc., the fortress of St. Augustine with everything which pertains to Florida, in order to prevent the shedding of Christian blood and the evil consequences which may result from the unrestrained fury of the several nations when they capture a plaza by force of arms. The British Camp in Florida. 20 June 1740 OS. James Oglethorpe—Vincent Pierse.

To Their Excellencies James Oglethorpe, General of the Army of His Britannic Majesty, and Vincent Pierse, Commodore of the warships and naval forces of His Britannic Majesty which at present are before the city of St. Augustine: We the undersigned Colonel Manuel de Montiano, Governor and Captain General of this city of St. Augustine and its provinces, Very Illustrious and Very Reverend Bishop of Tricale and Auxiliary Bishop of Cuba, officers and captains of the garrison of this plaza, in reply to the letter of summons of 20 June OS calling upon us to surrender this royal fortress and all that pertains to Florida to His Majesty George II, King of Great Britain, in order to prevent the shedding of Christian blood, we respond that we are entirely prepared and resolved to shed Christian blood in defense of this fort and this plaza to the glory of the sacred name of God and the honour of the armed forces of the King of all Spains, so that the dominion of His Majesty King Philip V our natural Lord may always prevail in them. St. Augustine, 2 July 1740 [NS]. Don Manuel de Montiano—Fray Francisco de San Buenaventura, Bishop of Tricale—Don Francisco Menéndez Marquez—Don Sebastián Sánchez—Don Ludovico Rodríguez Rozo—Don Miguel de Ribas—Don Fulgencio de Alfaros—Don Juan Durana—Don Isidro de León—Don Antonio Salgado—Don Féliz de Uriza Alonso—Don Alonso Izquierdo—Don Pedro Ramón Barrera—Don Pedro Lamberto Benedit Horruitiner—Don Sebastián López de Toledo—for my captain his lieutenant Don Antonio Izquierdo—for my captain Don Domingo Jacinto Rodríguez.[30]

In his letters to Güemes after the withdrawal of the English forces, Montiano thanked the governor of Havana particularly for having sent the six galliots which had been so useful to him. Montiano said that he had not yet been able to comprehend General Oglethorpe's conduct or his methods, and he marveled that with so strong a force the general should have ordered a retreat so precipitate as to abandon a wealth of provisions.[31] Montiano had resisted a temptation to pursue the English rear guard because his men were few and were very tired, and he did not wish to risk the ruin of the presidio after having saved it from disaster.[32]

Montiano thought that Oglethorpe's talk about a second siege might have been calculated to placate the Carolinians. He thought it unlikely that they would follow Oglethorpe a second time, and that any assistance the general might get from South Carolina would be slow. However, all the schemes of the citizenry of South Carolina and Georgia seemed to proceed from their desire to capture St. Augustine, since it was the obstacle which prevented them from exterminating the Indians of Apalache in order to occupy all of Florida unopposed. If their intense distrust of Oglethorpe continued, the Carolinians might petition their king to give the command to another soldier. On the other hand, Oglethorpe might be clever enough to bewitch them again. In any case, it was necessary that the St. Augustine garrison be strongly reinforced, because if there was another attack, it would be with at least twice the number of men. Montiano added, "I must immediately send a messenger to the Uchizes so that in view of all this intelligence they will release themselves from friendship and obedience to the English, and I shall promise to reward them well if they care to come to visit us."[33]

As a reward for his defense of St. Augustine, Montiano was praised by King Philip V and made a brigadier. Before the end of the War of Jenkins' Ear, however, the governor would be reprimanded by his superiors for the failure of his expedition against Georgia in 1742, and for not having taken action against Oglethorpe when he made his final ineffectual invasion of Florida in March 1743. By the end of Montiano's term of office in 1749, he had greatly improved the fortifications of St. Augustine and Apalache, had built a stone fort at Matanzas Inlet, and had made an alliance with the Uchize Indians which persisted until 1763, when Great Britain took possession of the province by treaty.

AILEEN MOORE TOPPING.

NOTES.

1. Dispatch to Don Thomás Geraldino, Madrid, 27 November 1737, Archivo General de Indias: Audiencia de Santo Domingo, Legajo 2592, Document 96 (hereafter cited as AGI:SD, followed by legajo and document numbers). Dates in the Spanish documents used in the introduction are from the Gregorian calendar (NS); those in the English documents are from the Julian (OS); the discrepancy between the two calendars at the time the documents were written was ten or eleven days.

2. Juan Francisco de Güemes y Horcasitas to the Marqués de Torrenueva, Havana, 18 April 1738, AGI: SD 2593/43.

3. Güemes to Don Joseph Patiño, Havana, 12 December 1736, AGI:SD 2591/58.

4. Geraldino to Torrenueva, London, 31 January 1737, AGI:SD 2592/5. Oglethorpe told Geraldino that he had left Georgia "in a perfect understanding with the

commandant of Florida." For useful studies of the Florida-Georgia territorial question one should consult Verne E. Chatelaine, *The Defenses of Spanish Florida, 1565–1763* (Washington, 1941); Verner W. Crane, *The Southern Frontier, 1670–1732* (Ann Arbor, Mich., 1929); John Jay TePaske, *The Governorship of Spanish Florida, 1700–1763* (Durham, N.C., 1964); J. Leitch Wright, Jr., *Anglo-Spanish Rivalry in North America* (Athens, Ga., 1971). A Spanish document recommended in the report of the Conde de Montijo to the Marqués de Torrenueva relative to Florida and Georgia affairs, San Lorenzo, 9 November 1737, AGI:SD 2592/92, 165 pp.

5. Real cédula, Madrid, 12 April 1737, AGI:SD 851/77.

6. Manuel de Montiano to the king, St. Augustine, 31 August 1738, AGI:SD 2541/47; Consejo de Indias to the king, Madrid, 14 February 1739, AGI:SD 838/44.

7. Güemes to Montiano, Havana, 24 March 1738 AGI:SD 2593/32.

8. Montiano to Güemes, St. Augustine, 14 August 1739, Library of Congress, East Florida Papers, Bundle no. 37, Letters of Montiano to the Captain General of Cuba, no. 156 (hereafter cited as EFP, 37, followed by letter number).

9. Güemes to Don Joseph de la Quintana, Havana, 18, 24 July 1739, AGI:SD 2593/59; enclosure: deposition of Juan Castelnau.

10. Montiano to Güemes, St. Augustine, 3 April 1739, EFP, 37, no. 133.

11. James Edward Oglethorpe to the Trustees of Georgia, Savannah, 5 October 1739, in *The Colonial Records of the State of Georgia*, ed. Allen D. Candler et al. (Atlanta, 1913), vol. 22, pt. 2, p. 217 (hereafter cited as CRG).

12. Oglethorpe to William Bull, Georgia, 27 September 1739, *The St. Augustine Expedition of 1740, A Re-*

port to the South Carolina General Assembly, Reprinted from the Colonial Records of South Carolina, with an Introduction by John Tate Lanning (Columbia, South Carolina Archives Department, 1954), appendix no. 1, p. 91 (hereafter cited as *Report*).

13. Güemes to the governor of South Carolina, Havana, 28 March 1738, a copy enclosed in Güemes to Torrenueva, Havana, 18 April 1738, AGI:SD 2593/34.

14. Oglethorpe to the Accountant Harman Verelst, Savannah, 9 October 1739, CRG, p. 231.

15. *Report*, pp. 10–18.

16. Ibid., introduction, pp. xii–xiv.

17. Joseph Ioor Waring, M.D., *James Killpatrick and Smallpox Inoculation in Charlestown, Annals of Medical History, New-Series* X (1938); Carolyn T. Moore, *Abstract of the Wills of the State of South Carolina 1670–1740,* vol. 2 (Charlotte, 1960), pp. 133, 143, 201–2, 229.

18. *Report*, introduction, p. xxvii.

19. Oglethorpe to Bull, British Camp in Florida, 19 July 1740, *Report*, appendix 129, pp. 169–70. For a useful analysis of the campaign see Phinizy Spalding, *Oglethorpe in America* (Chicago, 1977), pp. 110–26.

20. Journal of Don Domingo de la Cruz, 1740, AGI: SD 2584/28.

21. Pedro Ruiz de Olano to the king, St. Augustine, 8 August 1740, AGI:SD 2658/20.

22. Fray Francisco de San Buenaventura y Tejada to Dr. Joseph Ortigoza, St. Augustine, 1740 (Seville, Spain, 1740).

23. Montiano to Quintana, St. Augustine, 21 November 1739, AGI:SD 2584/18.

24. Montiano to the king, St. Augustine, 31 January 1740, AGI:SD 2658/8.

25. Montiano to Güemes, St. Augustine, 23 February 1740, EFP, 37, no. 190, no. 191.

26. Montiano to Güemes, St. Augustine, 25 March 1740, ibid., no. 192.

27. Montiano to Güemes, St. Augustine, 27 April 1740, AGI:SD 2658/11; EFP, 37, no. 193.

28. Montiano to Güemes, St. Augustine, 24 June 1740, EFP, 37, no. 200.

29. Copy of a paper found near Moze, 14 June 1740, AGI:SD 2658/23.

30. Montiano to the king, St. Augustine, 9 August 1740, AGI:SD 845/8; AGI:SD 2658/12; enclosures. At Moze, Colonel John Palmer was killed, but his son, Captain William Palmer, was not.

31. Montiano to Güemes, St. Augustine, 28 July 1740, AGI:SD 2541/55; EFP, 37, no. 205.

32. Montiano to Güemes, St. Augustine, 3 August 1740, EFP, 37, no. 207.

33. Montiano to Güemes, St. Augustine, 7 August 1740, AGI:SD 2658/20; EFP, 37, no. 210.

AN
Impartial Account
OF THE LATE
EXPEDITION
AGAINST
ST. AUGUSTINE
UNDER
General *Oglethorpe*.

Occasioned by

The *Suppression* of the REPORT, made by a Committee of the *General Assembly* in SOUTH-CAROLINA, transmitted, under the *Great Seal* of that Province, to their *Agent* in ENGLAND, in order to be printed.

WITH AN

Exact PLAN of the Town, Castle and Harbour of *St. Augustine*, and the adjacent Coast of *Florida*; shewing the *Disposition* of our Forces on that ENTERPRIZE.

The Suppression of Evidence is the strongest Evidence of Guilt.
TRENCHARD.

LONDON:
Printed for J. HUGGONSON, in *Sword-and-Buckler-Court*, over-against the *Crown-Tavern* on *Ludgate-Hill*, 1742.　(Price One Shilling)

The PREFACE.

THE Reason of publishing these Sheets being manifest from the Title Page, I shall not pretend to a Knowledge of those secret and extraordinary Motives, that could induce the Agent of a Province to dispense with the Directions of that Province, by suppressing their Sense of a public Affair, a very important one to them, and perhaps not without some Significance to the Kingdom itself. I have read it, and am convinc'd by common Sense, that it contains no Treason, nor affirms any thing without clear and sufficient Proof. And without doubt, the Legislature of that Province did not conceive the Publication of it to be a very indifferent Thing, either for their own Justification, or the Information of Great-Britain, when the Enquiries they enter'd upon in order to it, and the Digestion of the Report afterwards employ'd so much time there, and the Impression of it here must necessarily expose them to a farther Expence, when

A 2

they

they had but little Inclination to add to that extraordinary one, so fruitlesly advanced towards the Expedition.

But whatever Motives may have determined the Conduct of another in this Affair, a sincere Love of Truth, and a hearty Attachment to the general Interest of that Government that secures my just and natural Freedom, are the real Causes of my endeavouring to obviate any Evils that might arise from the Suppression of so seasonable an Information as that Report might have furnished our Superiors with. If any Errors shall appear in the Conduct of this Siege, the Representation of them is the surest Way to prevent their Repetition, if a second Attack should be enterpriz'd: And whatever Steps of it may be approv'd, will naturally recommend themselves to those such Enterprize shall be committed to. Besides, as a Spirit of Enquiry into public Affairs seems to prevail now, and will, no doubt, be attended with proper and speedy Measures for rectifying whatever needs it; it was imagin'd that no Juncture could ever prove more seasonable and critical than the present, for tendering this Narrative to the Public.

This

This Pamphlet may justly be consider'd as a very fair Abstract of that full and authentic Report, whose Suppression has produc'd it. The chief Difference is, that the Report contains much more, several Examinations, Depositions, and Proofs being annexed to it, which this has not. However to give a right Idea of this, the Author is satisfied it contains the greatest Part of the material Facts mentioned in the Report; the Narrative of the Expedition is nearly in the same Terms; and the Reflexions on the same Measures, frequently similar, as they naturally must. No Proof or Paper is cited in this, of which the Relator has not, by the Favour of Friends, seen the Original, or authentic Copies. And if he has ever set down any thing upon other Information or Rumour, he has specified such Information or Rumour as the Foundation of it.

It is not expected that a Thing of this Nature can escape the Censure of those who will imagine themselves or their Friends affected by it: Nevertheless the Relator thinks he is not without Reason in calling it, An impartial Narrative, since he has strictly related such Facts as he had a regular Information of; and

his

his Reflexions on them appear to himself so obvious and unstrained, that he must have made the same on the same Facts, if every Person concerned in them had been unknown to him. That others of equal Impartiality and better Judgment, may justly differ from him in many of them may be owing to his Incapacity, but not to any sinister Intention. He has at least the good Fortune of having a little Intimacy with his abundant Defects, he has not the least Enmity against any Person mentioned in the Affair, and is at this time as little interested about that Expedition as most of his Readers.

In brief, whoever is offended with this Narrative, must be at Enmity with Truth: Tho' when Facts are extravagant and unaccountable, the most impartial Relator of them contracts an Air of Prejudice with superficial Readers, and even People of Discernment, who are affected by it, will at least consider him as officious, and tell him, that when he had confessed so little Interest in the Affair, he might have left it to those who had more. To this the Answer is obvious, that in all disputed Cases it is the real Duty of every Man, to contri-
bute

bute whatever he knows towards the Attainment and Difcovery of Truth, efpecially where he has been a *Witnefs* to any ungenerous Endeavour to fupprefs it, whether he is called upon or not, or whether he has any Intereft or no in the Difcovery: Nay, the lefs he is affected by the Iffue, he is the better qualified for an impartial Evidence. Whatever the Sentiments of fuch may be, who make SELF the invariable Rule of Conduct, a Promptitude to this cannot be impertinent in any Man, and it were well for every Community if a greater Majority were of fuch an honeft, generous Difpofition.

If I fhould be inadvertently guilty of mifreprefenting any thing, I know there is the authentic Senfe of a large Committee of no inconfiderable Province, properly exemplify'd in the Hands of their Agent, who may convict me of fuch Difagreement by printing it. And if the Facts herein afferted fhall be fairly difprov'd, the Relator will think himfelf obliged by Truth and Honefty to acknowledge his Miftakes, and to declare the Reafons that enforced him to receive them for Truths. This indeed he has not the leaft Apprehenfion he fhall be reduced to; but if

ever

ever he is, he will observe his Engagement with a sensible Satisfaction. For notwithstanding the Multitude of Contentions in the World, nothing but Truth and Liberty can be worth the Contention of a considerate Man, and Liberty indeed, as it is Truth. And wherever the Ambition of others attempts to invade and efface that natural, popular Truth, they should be considered as the wanton and wicked Enemies of Human Nature it self, and be entitled to as little Quarter from the Species, as those Beasts who are sometimes so by Necessity.

I need not inform any military Reader who may peruse this Trifle, that the Relator is not of that honourable Profession. My want of proper Terms, and perhaps of proper Observations, will make it but too evident. I hope it may appear intelligible ; and if the Performance can pretend to any Excellence, it is owing to its Truth, a Circumstance very favourable to the Author's many Defects ; as it needs very little Capacity to illustrate, very little Elegance to adorn it.

Ipsa suis pollens opibus, nihil indiga nostri.

A NAR-

A Narrative *of the* CON-DUCT *of the Forces on the Expedition against* St. Au-GUSTINE.

IN order to conceive the cleareſt Idea of this unfortunate Affair, and to evince the real Importance of it, it ſeems requiſite to attend a little to the Motives that induced the Province of *South-Carolina* to engage in an Expedition againſt the Town and Caſtle of *St. Auguſtine.* The Reſolutions and Meaſures they entered on in Conſequence of ſuch Motives, will, next be related. To which a juſt and ſuccinct Enumeration of the Steps this Enterprize was conducted with in the Field will neceſſarily ſucceed: And ſome fair unſtrained Reflexions on the moſt evident Cauſes of this unhappy Diſappointment, will naturally conclude this *Impartial* Enquiry on the Subject.

It ſeems no ways neceſſary here to deſcend to every minute Inconvenience, the Province received from the Neighbour-

B   hood,

hood of that Garriſon in its early Settlement, nor to ſpecify what particular Perſons were ſenſibly injured by it. The
Expedition of Colonel *James Moore* againſt
it in 1702, is ſufficient to convince us,
that the *Carolinians* were very ſenſible then
of their Inſecurity from it; when the Settlement, leſs extended and populous than
at preſent, undertook the Siege of it with
a ſmaller Number of Troops than were
on this Expedition, and without any Bombs
or Veſſels of Force to prevent the arrival
of Supplies, which two Defects ſeem to
have been the ſole Reaſons of their Diſappointment then, as they entirely deſtroyed
the Town, and drove all the Inhabitants
into the Caſtle, with little or no Loſs on
their Part. Indeed, on this Occaſion they
entrenched on the Main, and cloſe about
the Town, having their little Force together, and not being ſeperated by Water, a
Mile or two from the Garriſon they beſieged.

And about twelve or thirteen Years ago,
after ſome Miſchief done by thoſe *Indians*,
they corrupted and protected, Colonel
Palmer, with about 300 Men, to the beſt
of

of my Recollection, a great part of whom were *Indians*, deſtroyed and plundered the Town ; driving all the Inhabitants into the Caſtle, killing ten or twelve *Yamaſees*, and returning without Loſs to *Charles Town.* Indeed their Booty was never conſiderable enough to prove a Motive for ſuch Attempts ; but as that Garriſon, even in Times of Peace, was a continual Receptacle of criminal and fugitive Slaves, who might prove very injurious to *Carolina*, as Guides and Pilots to the *Spaniards* in Times of Hoſtility ; and as they were continually doing their utmoſt to corrupt the *Indians*, and encourage the Slaves to deſert with the Hopes of Freedom, *&c.* it became neceſſary for that Province to ſecure themſelves by the earlieſt Precautions from ſuch evil Conſequences, as the diſhoneſt Conduct of ſuch a Neighbour might produce. There was formerly a Stipulation between them, by which the Garriſon obliged themſelves to give up every fugitive Slave that ſhould run there ; but this was ſoon evaded, as they ſaid they were made *Chriſtians*, and become the King of *Spain's*

 Subjects ;

Subjects; and those who could obtain any Confideration for their Slaves, were obliged to accept a pecuniary one, and they were but a few who ever had that.

When we reflect that Rice, the chief Staple of *Carolina*, is manufactured by Negroes, (*European* Conftitutions being really unequal to the Culture of it in that Climate, or indeed to the general Culture of the Climate) it muft be evident, that a great Number of Slaves are neceffary to produce the yearly Quantities of that and other Commodities exported from that Province; and, without entering into a ftrict Calculation, it is certain they greatly out-number the white People there. Now, if, even in Times of Peace with *Spain*, they have been harraffed with Infurrections and Maffacres from them, what can they expect in cafe of an Invafion, when their Enemies would certainly encourage their Revolt; and what Refiftance could a thin, yet valuable Colony make to a Foe without, when they had fuch numerous and cruel ones within, at whofe Mercies the Lives of their Families muft lie, upon

their

their exerting any rigorous Oppofition againft the publick Enemy. In fhort, if it be confidered, that the late Expedition was undertaken immediately after the great Mortality of the Years 1738 and 39, by the Small Pox and bilious Fevers, and how much a thin Colony, and not in its moft flourifhing Circumftances, contributed, by their Perfons and Fortunes, in hopes of reducing that Fortrefs, their Senfe of the Neceffity of reducing it muft have been very ftrongly expreffed in the Meafures they entered on for that Purpofe.

It cannot furprize us, that a People fo peculiarly circumftanced fhould liften very favourably to every Propofal, and fhould be inclined to hope the beft from every Argument that was ufed as a further Incitement to fuch an Undertaking: For, however heartily they muft defire the Removal of fo inconvenient a Neighbour, fo ungenerous an Enemy, they were convinced their fingle Power was infufficient to diflodge him. But what firft engaged their publick Deliberations on this Subject, was a Letter from his Excellency General *Oglethorpe,*

thorpe, dated *September* 21, 1739, to the Honourable *William Bull*, Eſq; Lieutenant-Governor of that Province, wherein he acquaints him, " That he had re-
" ceived Orders from his Majeſty to an-
" noy the Subjects of the King of *Spain*
" in the beſt Manner he was able ; and
" that he hoped the People of *Carolina*
" would give the neceſſary Aſſiſtance,
" that they might begin with the Siege of
" *Auguſtine*, before more Troops arrived
" from *Cuba*." The Contents of which being communicated to the Commons Houſe of Aſſembly, by the Lieutenant-Governor, in a Meſſage on the 8th of *November* following, a Committee was appointed to take the ſame under Conſideration, who, in their Report thereon recommended, " That, in caſe General
" *Oglethorpe* ſhould think proper to form
" a Deſign of beſieging *Auguſtine*, and
" ſhould communicate his Scheme to the
" General Aſſembly, and ſhould make it
" appear, that the ſame might probably
" be attended with Succeſs, that then the
" Publick of this Province wou'd en-
" gage

" gage to give General *Oglethorpe* the beſt
" Aſſiſtance they reaſonably could, to put
" his Scheme in Execution."   To this
the Houſe agreed, and, in Conſequence
thereof, ſent a Meſſage to the Upper Houſe,
" to deſire their Concurrence, and that
" they would apply to the Governor to
" communicate the ſame to General *Ogle-*
" *thorpe*".

On the 4th of *February* following, the
Lieutenant-Governor ſent down to the
Lower Houſe an Account of the Aſſiſtance
the General expected from this Province,
conſiſting of ſuch Forces, Preſents for *In-*
dians, Ammunition, Proviſions for ſuch
Forces, and for 400 *Men of his own Re-*
giment for three Months, and ſuch other
Stores as he thought reaſonable and neceſſary for this Province to furniſh towards
the Siege.   Which Propoſal having been
conſidered by a Committee of both Houſes, they reported, " That the ſame would
" exceed the Sum of 200,000 Pounds
" *Carolina* Currency, which they were of
" Opinion was too large an Expence for
" the Province to bear ; but recommend-
" ed

" ed that, if the General would under-
" take the Expedition againſt *St. Auguſtine,*
" and would certify to the General Aſſem-
" bly of the Province, that the ſame was
" likely to be attended with the Succeſs
" of taking that Garriſon, with ſuch an
" Aſſiſtance from this Province, as ſhould
" not exceed 120,000 Pounds; that the
" Publick of this Province were willing
" to be at that Expence, and would pro-
" vide for the ſame;" which was agreed
to by the Houſe.   And that Committee
being directed to calculate, what Number
of Forces, what Preſents for *Indians,* what
Proviſions, *&c.* might be tranſported to
Auguſtine for that Sum, reported, " That
" the ſame was ſufficient for a Regiment
" of Foot, containing eight Companies
" of 60 Men each; for 300 Pioneers,
" Preſents for 1000 *Indians,* and Proviſi-
" ons for the Whole for ſix Months."
This was alſo communicated to the General by the Lieutenant Governor, at the
Requeſt of both Houſes, together with
certain Articles propoſed to be ſtipulated
with the General, for conducting the Expedition.   The

The General coming soon after to *Charles Town*, desired the Lieutenant-Governor, in a Letter of *March* 26, 1741, to acquaint the Assembly, " That he had re-
" ceiv'd their Plan, proposing the Assi-
" stance of 120,000 Pounds towards the
" Siege of *Augustine*, and that he was
" come to consult Measures with them,
" for bringing that Enterprize to a happy
" Conclusion, with the smallest Expence
" of Men and Money.   For which Pur-
" pose it would be best immediately,
" with what Men could be had, to make
" a SUDDEN ATTEMPT."   And on the 29th of the same Month, the Lieutenant-Governor sent down to the Commons House of Assembly, the General's Plan of Assistance, for a *sudden Attack* upon *Augustine*; proposing, " That
" one Regiment of 400 Men should be
" raised, a Troop of Rangers or Cattle
" Hunters, Presents for 500 *Indians*, Pro-
" visions for the Whole for three Months,
" and Arms, Ammunition, Tools and
" Utensils, adding, that unless the same
" could be furnished so as to set out from

C   " *Charles-*

" *Charles-Town* in fourteen Days, the En-
" terprize would not be likely to fuc-
" ceed."   It was the unanimous Opinion
of the Houfe, upon confidering thefe Pro-
pofals, " That the Particulars therein fpe-
" cified could not poffibly be provided
" by this Government in fo fhort a Term."
And as they had then the greateft Reafon
to think the Enterprize would be declined,
they directed their Committee to join a
Committee of the Upper Houfe, and de-
fired the General might be asked, " What
" Supplies he thought would be neceffary
" to keep the War on the other Side of
" St. *John*'s River.

There was accordingly a Conference of
a large Committee of both Houfes the
fame Day, at which the General and Capt.
Vincent Pearfe, Commodore of his Ma-
jefty's Ships of War in thofe Parts, and
moft of the Members of both Houfes
were prefent. When the General propofing
to the Committee to ftay a longer Time for
the Supplies, and reprefenting to them,
" That he had private Intelligence from
" *Auguftine*, that they were in the greateft
" Want

" Want of Provisions; that he was cer-
" tain many of the Garrison would de-
" sert, and that he did not doubt making
" himself Master of the Town the FIRST
" NIGHT: That the Multitude of Wo-
" men and Children who would be forced
" from thence into the Castle, must ne-
" cessarily distress it; which, being fol-
" lowed with the throwing in of several
" Bombs, would undoubtedly produce a
" speedy Surrender: That in case the *Ha-*
" *vanna* was taken, the *Spaniards* would
" in all Probability, rather call in the
" *French* to *Augustine,* than let it fall in-
" to our Hands." In brief, both he and
the Commodore giving the greatest En-
couragement to the Committee to report
in Favour of the Enterprize, the latter of
whom said, " they ought all to be hang'd
" if they did not take it in a very short
" Time; and the General further repre-
senting, " that he had sent for several *In-*
" *dians* who were daily expected down
" to the Expedition," the Committee induced by such Reasons, recommended it
in their Report, " to assist him with such

 " Forces

" Forces and Neceſſaries as were thought
" ſufficient to the Enterprize, according
" to his own Plan laſt mentioned, and
" to continue the ſame for one Month
" longer than he had propoſed;" being
only prevented from continuing them
for ſix Months in the Whole, by the
Captains of his Majeſty's Ships declaring,
" they could not venture to ſtay ſo long,
" as they apprehended the Hurricane Sea-
" ſon would approach before the Expi-
" ration of that Term." All which being approved by both Houſes, an Act
was paſſed, *April* 5, 1741, for carrying
the ſame into Execution.

These Engagements were not only punc-
tually fulfilled by that Province, except
the Article of Rangers, who could not be
procured, and indeed could have been of
no important Service, but leaſt they ſhould
not prove ſufficient for the End propoſed,
the Aſſembly afterwards voted an Addition
of 200 Men more for it. Beſides which,
the Lieutenant-Governor purchaſed by their
Allowance, a large Schooner with ten
Carriage and 16 Swivel Guns, in which
they

they put 50 Men under the Command of Capt. *Tyrrell*, and having thus even exceeded the General's laſt Demands, they pleaſed themſelves with the agreeable Proſpect of Succeſs, no ways doubting his Excellency's Zeal and Capacity for his Majeſty's Service, and the Security and Happineſs of his Fellow Subjects in *Georgia* and *Carolina*.

The Contributions of *South Carolina* towards this Enterprize, being thus ſpecify'd, the Meaſures purſued at the Siege, or in the Field, demand our next Conſideration. It appears then by the ſeveral Letters and Papers ſent by the General and Col. *Vanderduſſen*, who commanded the *Carolina* Regiment, and by the Examinations of the Colonel, the Lieutenant-Colonel and Major of the ſaid Regiment, and ſeveral other Gentlemen employed in that Expedition, (the proper Extracts of which and all other neceſſary Proofs, are contained in the Appendix of the Report, under the Sanction of the publick Seal of the Province, now in the Hands of their Agent, Mr. *Fury*,) that the Place of Rendezvous was at the Mouth of *St. John's* River,

River, on the *Florida* Shore, where the General arrived with his Forces, a Detachment of the *Carolina* Regiment, and the *Cherokee Indians* on the 9th of *May* ; from whence they marched on the 10th, to attack Fort *Diego*, about 20 Miles diftant, which Fort had 9 Swivel, 2 Carriage Guns of two Pound Shot, and 50 Men. And having furrounded it on the 12th, they fent in a *Spanifh* Prifoner with a Drum, to fummon the Garrifon, who immediately capitulated on the following Conditions. The Garrifon to furrender Prifoners of War, and deliver up the Fort with the Guns and Stores to the King of *Great-Britain*. 2*dly*, That they fhould have Liberty to keep their Baggage, and not be plundered. 3*dly*, That Seignior *Diego Spinofa*, to whom the Fort belonged, being built at his Expence, and on his Lands, fhould hold his Lands, Slaves, and fuch other Effects, as were not already plundered in the Field. 4*thly*, That no Deferters or Runaways from *Carolina*, fhould have the Benefit of this Capitulation, but be furrendered at Difcretion. This Fort was garrifoned by 60 of the General's Forces,

and

and from thence they returned to the Place of Rendezvous, where they were joined by Colonel *Vanderduſſen* with the reſt of the *Carolina* Regiment on the 19th of *May*, whence they marched again to *Diego* the 31ſt, and from thence in two Days to Fort *Mooſa*, in View of, and near two Miles diſtant from *Auguſtine*, and 23 from *Diego*.

The *Spaniards* having deſerted *Mooſa*, the General ordered the Gates to be burnt, and three Breaches to be made in the Walls. They then proceeded with the whole Army to reconnoitre the Town and Caſtle, after which they returned back to *Diego*. From thence the General ordered Colonel *Vanderduſſen* to march with his Regiment, and take Poſſeſſion of Point *Quartell*, lying to the *North* of the Bar, and ſeparated from Fort *Mooſa* by a Creek; while the General with about 260 Men of his Regiment, and the greateſt part of the *Indians* embarked on Board the Men of War, and arrived at the Iſland of *Anaſtatia*, oppoſite to the Caſtle; leaving behind him on the Main, but between 90 and 100 white Men, *Highlanders* and others in his Pay, with

with 42 *Indians* and two commiſſioned Officers, to alarm the *Spaniards* on that Side, as he ſaid; but gave a verbal Command of the Whole to Colonel *Palmer*, a Volunteer from that Province. About the ſame Time 200 Sailors from the Ships were landed upon that Iſland, which the *Spaniards* directly abandoned, under the Command of Captain *Warren*, Captain *Laws*, and the Honourable Captain *Townſhend*, who were all very inſtrumental, by their exemplary Courage and Diligence in inciting their Men to erect Batteries, and do ſuch other Services as preſented.

While the Troops were thus diſpoſed, a ſtrong Detachment iſſued from the Caſtle of *Auguſtine*, *June* 15, between three and four in the Morning; and attacking the Party under the Command of Colonel *Palmer*, then at Fort *Mooſa*, defeated them, killing the Colonel, with ſeveral others, and taking many Priſoners, after which the *Carolina* Regiment was ordered over to *Anaſtatia*.

Two Batteries were thrown up on the Iſland of *Anaſtatia*, one a Mile and Quarter, the

the other a Mile and Half, and a Third at *Point Quartel*, a Mile and Quarter from the Castle of *Augustine*. From these Batteries they fired at the Castle and Town, and threw off a great Number of Shells. The Fire was returned from the Castle, and from six *Spanish* Half Gallies in the Harbour that chiefly annoyed our Forces: Upon which it was proposed to attack the Gallies, and was agreed to by the 3 Sea Commanders ashore, and such of the Land-Officers as consulted with them, and a Time was appointed to put it in Execution. But the final Omission of this important Service will be more properly mentioned, when we come to relate the Conduct of the Maritime Forces assembled on this Expedition.

Soon after this, the Garrison received a Supply of Provisions, *&c.* from *Cuba*, which was discovered by Capt. *Fanshaw*, of his Majesty's Ship *Phœnix*, after they were got within the *Mosquito's*; from whence they were conveyed up the *Mettanfas*, and landed to the Southward of the Town, where there was no Battery to

D

annoy,

annoy, or Force to intercept them. And now the Season of the Year approaching, in which the Captains of the King's Ships supposed it might be dangerous to continue on the Coast, they resolved to sail on the 5th of *July*, and in order thereto, commanded their Men from *Anastatia* on Board. Whereupon the General, *July* 4. sent Orders to Col. *Vanderdussen*, and Lieutenant-Colonel *Cooke*, to raise the Blockade, and bring off the Train and Troops, with the least Loss they could; and to spoil the Artillery if they could not fetch it off. Accordingly the Colonels made a Retreat, carrying off every thing entire, but one Cannon which was split, tho' the General burnt a great Quantity of Provisions, Arms, &c. on his Retreat, notwithstanding there were two empty Boats at hand, which might have carry'd them off. After this Col. *Vanderdussen* joined the General's Regiment on the Main, from whence they retreated to *St. John's*; several of the General's Regiment having deserted. And thus ended this most disgraceful and unfortunate Expedition.

Upon

" Upon the Colonel's expreſſing his great Diſſatisfaction at this mortifying Retreat, the General told him and another Gentleman then preſent, that he had done all that was expected from his Orders, and offered to ſhew them; intimating, that the Deſign was only to draw the *Spaniards* Attention from *Cuba.* But as well as I can remember, they told me, they did not give themſelves the Trouble to ſee them. I confeſs I ſhould have had the Curioſity, and poſſibly ſuch extraordinary Orders may even be worth the Inſpection of our Superiors. Nor indeed can it be ſuppoſed at all improbable from the whole Conduct of this Affair, that it was influenced by ſuch Orders, for as I remember, the Committee very juſtly obſerve, " That " from the Day the General left *Charles-* " *Town,* to that memorable Day of his " appearing with his Forces before *Au-* " *guſtine,* every Step he took had a ma- " nifeſt Tendency to alarm the Place be- " forehand, and to prevent that Surprize, " that was the profeſſed Deſign, and on " which, they greatly depended for Succeſs.

D 2

This

This I had from both these Gentlemen. And if this Siege were in Truth but a Feint, might not that have been effected without such an Expence to a Colony, who had appropriated her Rum Duty, and made other considerable Contributions to the Benefit of *Georgia*, on its first Settlement?

Tho' it may be supposed this brief Detail of the Enterprize will present many obvious Errors to an intelligent Person, without any particular Animadversions, yet is it difficult for the most indifferent Relator to suppress the Reflections which occur spontaneously on this Occasion. Our Minds are constituted in such a Manner, that it seems scarcely in our Election, whether we will reflect or not, on Subjects important in themselves, or their Consequences, when we have once enter'd on them. But in such Cases, we are to have the same inviolable Regard to Justice in our Observations, that we must to Truth in our Narrative. And still there will be this material Difference, that Facts, upon due Proof, must be admitted by every Person;

Person; tho' the Reflections of different Minds upon the same Facts, will frequently vary. Notwithstanding which, he may be consider'd, methinks, as a fair Animadverter, who utters no Remarks but such as appear to himself to result necessarily from such Facts, in the very Nature and Reason of Things; who can divest himself of every partial Prepossession and Prejudice, and considers the Actions rather than the Actors. 'Tis possible, I may very partially Mistake this to be my own Case, but I am certain and conscious it is my Desire and Endeavour that it should. No Man can well be supposed willing to deceive himself, where he can acquire nothing but Discredit by it; and I should judge it a real Immorality to intend the Deception of another. Some Readers who might not consider the Subject as interesting enough for their Reflexions, may yet be willing to hear another's; and those who shall judiciously disapprove mine, will make such as appear juster to themselves.

'Tis too certain indeed, that the best Reflexions in the present Case, are but a

kind

kind of *Phrygian* Wisdom, and incapable of preventing the Evils the adjacent Colonies may be expofed to from this Difappointment. For as the Vicinity of *Auguftine* can be no bad Reafon for difallowing Negroes in *Georgia*, fo any Perfon, generally acquainted with thofe Climates, may venture to affirm, that *Georgia* can fcarcely make a Figure, as a Colony, without them. And the Defertion of the *Carolina* Slaves, may not improbably be further increafed by this impotent Attempt upon that Fortrefs, whereby our Arms are certainly become contemptible both to them and the neighbouring *Indians*. Yet if it fhall appear, upon a fair Difquifition, that this Enterprize was not defeated by any fuch Events as were fortuitous, and could not eafily be forefeen or prevented ; but that it evidently refulted from our own Overfight or Mifconduct, a plain Eviction of the particular Errors muft effectually prevent a Repetition of them upon any future Revival of the like Attempt. Other Errors may occur, for who is infallible ? The fame fcarcely can,

and

and many Persons who have carefully considered these, have conceived it difficult
to devise others, that could in any wise
resemble a Siege, and operate so directly
to the Disappointment of it.

First then it appears, that the taking
Fort *St. Francis de Pupa*, wherein were 12
Soldiers and a Serjeant, before any Measures were concerted with the Province of
South-Carolina, for the Siege of *Augustine*,
was a very unseasonable Step, which served
only to Alarm the *Spaniards*, and put
them on the speediest Methods of con-
sulting their future Security. This was
proved beyond all Dispute by the Letters
found on Board a *Spanish* Vessel bound
from *St. Augustine* to *Cuba*, taken by Capt.
Warren; in one of which, the *Spanish* Governor relates the taking this very Fort,
and his daily Expectation of a Siege; pres-
sing for an immediate Supply of Provisi-
on, Ammunition, *&c.* to enable him to
maintain the Place. And in Consequence
of this early Alarm, those Supplies finally
arrived, which determined the Besiegers to
abandon the Enterprize. Yet this Over-
sight,

fight, however material, might probably have been redeemed by a proper Vigour in the Field afterwards, as it appeared by some intercepted Letters from the Governor of *Augustine* to the Commander of *St. Marks*, about 100 Miles beyond *St. Augustine*, that they had not above three Days Bread at the Arrival of those Supplies; which they considered as a miraculous Deliverance effected by *St. Rosana*, or the *Virgin* of the *Apalaches*.

It may well be supposed, that landing the Forces at the Mouth of *St. John's River*, and marching them thence to *Augustine* by Fort *Diego*, which was about 45 Miles very bad Way, where they were obliged to leave a 4 Pounder behind them, was very injudicious, in Comparison to landing them at *Pupa*, which is about 15, and a very good Road. Undoubtedly at such a hot Season of the Year, and in a Climate so generally intemperate and sickly during that Season, good Conduct and Humanity must have suggested the Necessity of easing the Army, as far as might be, without Detriment to the Service. And indeed it appears by
Colonel

Colonel *Barnwell*'s Examination, that the General acknowleged to him, " he was " advised in *Carolina* to rendezvous them " there, as the properest Place." And this was the Advice of such Gentlemen there, as were best acquainted with the Situation of *Augustine*, and the adjacent Country. The Reason assigned in Justification of this March of 30 Miles extraordinary, is really frivolous, *viz.* " Lest the Forces should " be discouraged for want of seeing the " Men of War" It is difficult to conceive that a Body of Veterans, or of any Soldiers, should be dejected by a short Separation from Vessels, which they must be satisfied, were engaged in, and actually had proceeded on the Expedition; especially as no Weather intervened to endanger or delay their Arrival. But it is undeniably clear, that many such hasty, unprofitable Marches (to give them the mildest Name) had greatly enfeebled and dispirited the Soldiery, when some of them dy'd under the Fatigue, and others were utterly unable to proceed; especially as there were continual Complaints of miserable Oeconomy,

E   and

and a moſt ſcanty Diſtribution of Proviſions to them. Humanity to our Fellow
Creatures and Fellow Subjects might be
thought a ſufficient Motive for a generous
Mind to allow no Ground for Diſſatisfaction and Complaints of this Nature;
or a very Zeal for the Service ſhould prevent ſuch ſevere Hardſhips, in time of
Action, as muſt be deſtructive of it. Yet
is it in Truth notorious, that there were
continual Complaints on this Occaſion in
the General's Regiment; and in Fact, it
appeared that theſe unneceſſary Marches
and unjuſt Reſtraint of Food was attended
with a very early Deſertion from the General's Regiment, whereby the Garriſon
was fully apprized of our Force and Diſ-
poſition. During this Campagne they
had no Leiſure to regale at their Victualling
Office, as the Oyſter Banks (very common in thoſe Countries, and very unwhole-
ſome in Summer) were familiarly called
by the Soldiers of *Frederica*. As his Excellency propoſed this for a SUDDEN
ATTEMPT, and was undoubtedly ſenſible, that Diſpatch and Secrecy are neceſſary

ceſſary to a Surprize, it is very difficult to reconcile ſuch ſeeming Hurry, and ſuch effectual Delay and impolitic Rigour with martial Skill and Foreſight. People who think they are very hardly dealt with, will often Hazard the Loſs of a very miſerable Life, for the meer Chance of bettering it. As on the other hand, thoſe who might have yielded to the firſt Impreſſions of their Fear and Panic, recollect their Judgment, and their Courage too, when they have a regular Apprehenſion of the Dangers that threaten them. We have already obſerved General *Oglethorpe* told the Committee of Conference, it was very likely he might carry the Town the FIRST NIGHT; and indeed by all Appearances it is probable he might, if he had then attempted it, when the whole Army, with which he reconnoitred it, expected that Service, and expreſs'd an Ardor for it. But inſtead of that we are told, " that himſelf and ſome other Officers " went up to the Walls, with ſeveral " Drums, and after alarming the Garri- " ſon, marched back to *Diego* with flying " Colours."

" Colours." 'Tis serioufly difficult to be grave on fuch an extraordinary Incident, fuch a fignificant Parade ! Were the Forces marched back to *Diego*, 25 Miles off, purely that they might meafure the fame Diftance thence again, to air and refresh them at this fultry Seafon ? For ought that appears here, they might have proceeded directly to entrench themfelves, to the *real* Inveftment of the Place, and Diftrefs of the Befieged. If fuch Meafures had a ferious Tendency to reduce this Fortrefs, it muft be acknowledged they were profound beyond Example; but People, who are unacquainted with the Depths of martial Policy, muft confider this loud Alarm, and *fudden Retreat* inftead of *Attempt*, as a Contrivance more likely to put the Garrifon on their Guard, than to furprize them. A March of 50 Miles muft have allowed them a convenient Leifure to recover from their Panic, and make them better prepared for a fecond Alarm. In fhort, to characterize fuch extraordinary Conduct with the ftricteft Propriety, we muft admit, it has more the Air of a Farce than of a Siege.   The

The Garrisoning and Guarding every insignificant Hut and Sandhill, and the frequent unnecessary Marches and Countermarches were nearly of the same Strain, being compar'd by an experienced and worthy Officer on the Spot, " to Squirrel " Hunting rather than War." As the Forces then under the General's Command were short of what he first proposed as necessary to the Enterprize, was it very consistent to weaken his little Army, by such frequent Detachments, however small? And as this was to be a SUDDEN ATTEMPT, how were such reiterated Motions and Counter-motions reconcileable with such an Intention? As they did make a circuitous March to *Augustine* by Fort *Diego*, it might very probably be prudent to take it in; if it were only, by the Capture of so many Prisoners, to deprive the Garrison of a Reinforcement of 50 Men, whenever they should incline to draw them thence. But it may be doubted, whether leaving a Detachment of 60 of our Men to Garrison it, was altogether prudent in our Circumstances. We find

this

this Fort 25 Miles from *Augustine* garrisoned, and further strengthned by a Ditch; but Fort *Moosa*, within two Miles of the Castle, dismantled. Now certainly we had less to apprehend at the former than the latter: The *Spaniards* would undoubtedly be more cautious of hazarding their Men at such a Distance, where Parties might interpose to cut them off, than where they had a continual View of the Place, and could receive an hourly Intelligence of our Force and Disposition. But it has been suggested, that garrisoning *Diego* was very commodious as a Place of Retreat; and we must acknowledge, that as Matters were afterwards conducted, it looked like a timely Precaution and Foresight.

Having already observed the Imprudence of retreating from the Town, which gave the *Spaniards* an Opportunity of entrenching round it, which we ought and neglected to do; the employing the main Body of the Troops on *Anastatia* and *Point Quartel*, may justly be considered rather as a necessary Consequence of that Neglect,

Neglect, than an original Blunder. The Castle could not readily be stormed from such a Disposition of the Troops, and as Lieutenant-Colonel *Cook*, an experienced Engineer and Officer, declared our Batteries too distant for any effectual Service, it was very unlikely they should ever be reduced to capitulate from thence. The *Spanish* Shot, which seemed generally well directed, fell frequently very near our Forces, but dead, and never killed or wounded one Man from the Castle. It was not then to be imagined that ours, from a like Distance, should batter heavy Walls to any Purpose. By this Distance of the Forces from the Castle, and their Separation from it, and from each other by Water, the whole Main was left open to the Besieged, if they might truly be called so, for themselves and their Cattle. Was this distressing them, or likely to produce the speedy Surrender so valiantly talked of? Did not this leave a free Passage to the Castle for any Supplies that should be landed on the Main? Whereas, if the Town had been carried, or even closely invested, and

a Bata Battery erected to the Southward of it, to command the River there, which Colonel *Vanderduſſen* propoſed, and Lieutenant-Colonel *Cook* approved to no Purpoſe, the Supplies that arrived, in ſpight of ſo many Men of War, muſt, with the greateſt Probability, have been either driven back, ſunk, or taken by the Beſiegers, as they were attended with no ſufficient Strength to force thro' them into the Place; in which Caſe it ſeems paſt doubt, that the Garriſon muſt be ſpeedily reduced to capitulate.

But if it were thought unadviſed or improper to hazard the Body of the Forces on the Main, 'tis hard to conceive the Prudence of ſending Colonel *Palmer* there, with leſs than 100 *Whites*, and but 42 *Indians*, within two Miles of the Caſtle, when the ſtronger Corps upon *Anaſtatia* and *Point Quartel*, were as ſecure from the Enemy as they were incapable of annoying them. Colonel *Barnwell* declared on his Examination, he heard Colonel *Palmer*, who was a good Judge of the Situation, tell the General, " the Party he
" ſent

" fent him over on the Main with, was
" took weak ; " but upon the General's
telling him " One of his Officers would
" undertake it with the fame Number,
" and that he would fend him over a
" Reinforcement when he had taken
" *Anaftatia* (which he never did) the
gallant Colonel accepted it, and proved
the Truth of his Affertion by the Defeat
of his Party, dying bravely himfelf, as
he had lived, in the Service of his Country. It has never been even fuggefted,
that any Meafures were ever taken to
have fupported this fmall Number in Cafe
of an Attack, tho' they were feparated by
Water, both from the General's and Colonel's Regiments, and the few who efcaped
being flain or taken Prifoners, owed their
Prefervation to a Boat that was acci-
dentally paffing by, which they hail'd
to fetch them over. Was it to be fuppofed they could continue to alarm the
Caftle frequently, for which it feems they
were fent there, without having their Numbers difcovered? And was it to be thought
the *Spaniards* would not determine, as they

F   did,

did, to cut them off by a superior Detachment, when they found them so effectually divided from the main Body? But we are told in the General's Letter, "That "this Misfortune happened thro' a Neg- "lect of those Orders by which they were "enjoined to encamp every Night in a "different Place." Was a Compliance with such Orders truly likely to have prevented this ill Event? Can it reasonably be supposed the Enemy was without *Spanish* or *Indian* Scouts, to discover their Force and Situation at so small a Distance? And these being once discovered, what availed it where a handful of Men encamped, that were daily employed to catch Horses at so much *per* Head, and had then caught about a Hundred? Must not their Fatigue enervate them for Action, compel them to sleep, and expose them to Surprize, as it actually happened? If the Castle was once taken, would not these precious Horses, and all the Stock have fallen of Course; and could it be prudent to harrass the Forces by an Employment that embarass'd the main Design? Were not

this

this small Party capable of making the same Defence at *Moosa* as elsewhere ? Nay, possibly if this Fort had not been unseasonably dismantled, they might have been able to repulse the Enemy. Ten *Creek Indians* who came to assist at the Siege, the Day before this Defeat, stopping at *Moosa*, asked Colonel *Palmer* where the General was ; and when he told them he was upon *Anastatia*, they asked him, " If the General sent them few Men " with their little Guns to fight against " so many Men, and such a strong Fort," saying, " They looked like something put " into a great Mouth, that was to be de- " voured as soon as the Mouth was shut." Common Reason made these untaught impolitick Savages true Prophets on this Occasion, which indeed required no Conjurer to foretel. Much might be added very pertinently, on the Madness or Barbarity of exposing such a small unsupported Party to such a superior Enemy ; but in brief, if it were intended to have sacrificed them, nothing less than a present Massacre could have done it more effectually.

F 2

Tho'

Tho' nothing can appear surprizing after such Conduct, I cannot avoid mentioning the Injustice and Imprudence of disgusting the *Indians* in Amity with the *English*, who had travelled so far to assist at the Siege. Some of the *Chickesaws* meeting with a *Spanish Indian* in one of their Excursions, killed him, and bringing his Head in Triumph to the Camp after their Manner, presented it to the General, who rejected it with Indignation, calling them "barbarous Dogs, and bid-"ding them be gone:" Upon which they said, "If they had carried the Head of "an *Englishman* to the *French*, they should "not be treated in that Manner." And *Squirrel*, their King, said, "If he had "carried one of our Heads to the Go-"vernor of *Augustine*, he should have "been used by him like a Man, as he "had been now used by the General like "a Dog." These very brave People, dreaded by the *French* and *Spaniards*, and our constant Friends, came to fight and assist in good Earnest at the Siege; nor could they be justly blamed, if it had been

all

all a Joke, for having never been let into it, they could never have dreamt of such a warlike Refinement. This Step so contrary to Justice and Policy, made them resolve to return Home; and it was at the earnest Intreaty and Instance of the *Carolina* Officers, they were prevailed on to stay. And this will appear the more unaccountable, when we recollect, that upon the Arrival of some *Indians* in the General's Camp, he wrote to Colonel *Vanderdussen* to send him some Presents for them, with a Power to distribute them, because (to use his own Words) " much " depends on the Nations." Certainly then some Indulgence to them was at least *necessary* ; and this extreme, romantic Tenderness, upon a due Consideration of all Circumstances, must have been truly injudicious and unseasonable.

What can be thought of the Capitulation of *Diego*, a Palisade Fort, whereby the Garrison were to be Prisoners of War, and the Cattle free and sacred, especially when his own Regiment had been so scantily subsisted before ? A *Carolina* Setler

and

and Soldier, who made bold with a Kidney of one of those who were said to be purchased from Signior *Diego*, very narrowly escaped Punishment for it, at the earnest Intercession of his Officers. They are used to Plenty of Meat in their own Country, and could not conceive the least Reason for being denied it in an Enemy's. It may be observed by the Way, that this same Signior, this *Diego*, was a *Negro* or *Mulatto*, who had been a considerable Time a Prisoner at large in the Camp, and whose Parole was afterwards taken for his Return from *Augustine*; but this Grand Person who had capitulated in such Form, and obtained such honourable Conditions for his Bullocks, forgot his personal Honour, and was content to be as cunning as those who depended on it. Two other *Spanish* Prisoners were sent into *Augustine* before this by the General, to induce the Garrison to desert, as he said, who never returned to inform us of their Success.

Many other Failures, tho' very evident and pernicious, are purposely omitted here; and indeed the Number and Magnitude of
these

these are less surprizing, when we observe they were not the Consequences of any Councils of War, but the sole Result of the Opinion and arbitrary Will of the Chief Commander, whose Orders were binding on all others.   He never called a single Council throughout the Expedition (for which it was well known in *Charles-Town* he quoted the Conduct of *Cæsar*) tho' his own Regiment contained brave Officers of undoubted Zeal and long Experience. And the *Carolina* Regiment desired nothing more than some right Plan of Action, in which they were prepared to co-operate at the utmost Hazard.   It is acknowledged, that in some Letters from the General to Colonel *Vanderdussen*, he tells him, " He " thanks him for his Advice, which will " always have great Weight with him, " and the like.   But how can we suppose this beyond meer Compliment, if it were not an Artifice, in some degree to co-lour over this gross Neglect of martial Councils.   It does not appear that the Measures pursued were the Advice of any other Officer, but it may be very confi-

dently

dently affirmed, that as many as had Judgment in such Affairs, and were zealous for the Success of this Expedion, constantly disapproved them : And some of the most experienced made an early Prediction of the ill Event, from the backward Steps that were made to a good one. But in Matters thus situated, who will venture to disobey or contend ? The Subordinate can only be safe in executing Commands they may observe with Reluctance, or by acquiescing to such Inaction as they must consider with Contempt. And whenever any Commander has lost the Confidence, the Esteem and Love of his Forces, what Good can be expected, what Evil may not be presumed, when his Courage against a publick Enemy may be restrained by his Horror of concealed ones ? Neither is it at all improbable that this Miscarriage might have been prevented by free Deliberation, and a timely Pursuit of different Councils. For it appears, that at a Conference in Colonel *Vanderduſſen's* Tent, on *Anaſtatia, June* 22, where besides himself and Lieutenant Colonel *Cook,*

Commo-

Commodore *Pearse*, Captain *Warren*, and Captain *Laws* were present, it was their unanimous Opinion, " That the General " rather retarded than forwarded Matters, " and that they should proceed with more " Vigour, when he was gone over on " the Main. " And indeed it appears that Captain *Warren* was very uneasy at his Conduct before, complaining, " that he " was not two Minutes of one Mind; " for which Reason he said, " he would " take no Notice of any but written Or-" ders from him, " adding, " That the " General was come there without any " Ammunition, Provisions, or other Ne-" cessaries but what he had from him, " which Lieutenant Colonel *Cook* very justly called, " a new System of War, and be-" ginning it at the wrong End. "

Having thus enumerated the principal Errors that occurred in the Management of the Land Forces, it remains to consider, with the same Truth and Impartiality, if any thing transacted or omitted by the Fleet may be judged to have contributed to this Disappointment.

Here

G

Here then we readily acknowledge that whatever Measures were taken, or not taken, seem in Consequence of some Consultation of the Commanders, and were founded on the Unanimity or Majority of the Board, which must in some Measure alter the Complexion of their Proceedings.

And first it seems, that not attacking the half Gallies, which are allowed to have chiefly affected our Forces, was an Error of great Importance. It appears that Commodore *Pearse*, in a Letter to Colonel *Vanderdussen*, of *June* 25, " recom-
" mends the Affair of attacking the Half-
" Gallies to the Consideration of the Sea
" Commanders on Shore ; and the Land
" Officers." In pursuance of which Recommendation, it appears, that *June* 26. a Conference was held in Colonel *Vanderdussen*'s Tent, where himself, Lieutenant. Colonel *Cook*, Capt. *Warren*, Capt. *Townshend*, and Capt. *Laws* being present, it was resolved to attack the Gallies provided there was Water enough on the *Swash* opposite to the Castle, for the Boats

to

to go round.   The same Afternoon Capt. *Warren* went on Board the Commodore, where a Counsel being held, the Result was, that the Thing was impracticable, of which Resolution, without annexing *one Reason* for it, the Commodore sent the General and the Colonel a Copy the same Evening ; and that Afternoon he also made a Signal for Capt. *Fanshaw*, who was cruizing off the *Metansas*, to come and join him.   To what Purpose can it appear, that the Commodore recommended this Affair to the Consideration of these Officers on Shore ?   Was it to approve his own Conduct in recommending it, if it had been disapproved there ? or to testify his extreme Caution, in getting it rejected, after they had resolved on the Execution of it ?

It appears further, that on *June* 27, between One and Two in the Morning, Capt. *Richard Tyrrel*, Commander of the Schooner belonging to *Carolina*, went in a Boat, and sounded between the Point and the Keys opposite to the Castle, and found four Feet on the North, and six on the

                    South

South End of the *Swash* at Half Flood, and returned safe without Discovery. Yet notwithstanding this Objection, as to the Depth of Water, being thus plainly removed, the same Day the Commodore sent Word to Colonel *Vanderdussen,* " he " would give no Assistance towards at- " tacking the Gallies, as thinking it " impracticable : " Upon which the Colonel went on Board the Commodore, and represented to the Captains assembled there, the bad Consequence of their going away without attacking them, but to no Purpose, the Majority voting it impracticable.

When it was first proposed to attack the Gallies, it appears to have been projected in the following Manner, *viz.* The General was to make a Diversion on the Main, by attacking the Town ; Colonel *Vanderdussen,* with Part of his Regiment, was to keep a continual Fire on the Town and Castle from the Batteries ; while Capt. *Tyrrel* was to have set upon the Gallies with the Seamen and the rest of the Colonel's Regiment. The General was accordingly

cordingly on the Main with his Troops, expecting that Service: But the Commodore difapproving this; and it being yet a fecond Time agreed to be attempted, upon the Remonftrances of Colonel *Vanderduffen* and Capt. *Warren*, when the Commodore's Lieutenant was to have commanded the Attack, new Difficulties were further ftarted when they came on Shore, and fo it was ftill unattempted. Yet it appears that foon after the Men of War flipping their Cables, and putting out to Sea in a Storm, the Colonel endeavoured to revive the Attempt on the Gallies in their Abfence. But propofing it to the Commodore's Lieutenant, Mr. *Swanton*, who appeared to be a Gentleman of Spirit, and commanded the Seamen left on Shore, he was told, " He had Orders " left not to venture any of them before " the Return of the Shipping."

It feems but too evident, that there was an exceffive Care to avoid any Hazard here, on this very important Service; and that it coft fome Pains and Trouble to elude the Refolution of the brave Sea Com-

Commanders on Shore and the Land Officers. 'Tis granted, that extreme Temerity must necessarily be restrained, notwithstanding the surprizing Success that has sometimes attended it: But surely Men that profess to assail and offend, may be also over cautious in War, where many Difficulties are ever supposed to be encountered, and Courage is to be exercised. This Attack was always judged not only practicable, but very likely to succeed by the Land Officers and the Commanders of the Ships who were ashore. The Seamen expressed their wonted Ardour for this Service, as well as the Land Forces, who were to join them in it; and the *Spaniards* were like to be so warmly employed on all Hands, that it was but a reasonable Presumption they might have prov'd too weak somewhere. This would at least have manifested a Disposition to act from some Quarter, and have shewn t hat the Lethargy ashore had not infected the Fleet: The Force of these Half Gallies, as they are rightly called, consists in one Nine Pounder in the Bow, called a Cashue

shue Piece, and some Swivel Guns fore
and aft. They have 20 Oars, and may
be supposed to have had about 30 Men
each. Besides, if the Six had been judged too formidable, there was a Juncture,
when three of them were separated two
Days from the rest. But upon a mature
Consideration of the Force and Manner
of the proposed Attack, it must needs
appear a strange Omission, and the more
so, as the Commodore contributed greatly
to this Expedition, by strongly encourag-
ing the Committee of Conference to report in Favour of it, and making light
of all the Difficulties that should arise in
the Progress of it. But this indeed was
the Conference.

I believe it will be thought universally
surprizing, that seven of his Majesty's Ships
of War and the Country Schooner were
insufficient to intercept, or keep off the Supplies that arrived, notwithstanding there was
an Information by two Deserters, that the
Garrison expected them; especially when we
consider that the Country Schooner which
remained within the Harbour, was purchased

chafed exprefly for the Purpofe of guarding the Inlet to the Southward of the Town, and the Paffage of thofe Supplies through the Harbour of *Auguftine* was fufficiently obviated by the Batteries on *Anaftatia,* and Point *Quartel.* At the fame time it is not to be doubted but the refpective Commanders of the King's Ships, or the Commanding Officer of each in their Abfence on fhore, difpofed their Ships and Motions in due Obedience to their proper Orders. And yet furely their Difpofition or Inattention muft have been very unaccountable, and it is hard to conceive what could intervene to have prevented fome of them from falling in with thofe Supplies, if there had been any tolerable Vigilance and Affiduity. But fome have imagined there might not have been a requifite Number of Captains to form proper Councils of War, if they had been employ'd on the cruizing which muft be confidered as a principal Reafon for their being ordered before the Place. And this moft material Neglect, which determined the Enterprize, was the more unexpected,

as

as the Commodore affured the Committee of Conference, " He would anfwer for " it, that the Place fhould have no Re- " lief by Sea."

Neverthelefs as thofe Supplies which got into the *Mufquito's*, were afterwards tranf-ported thro' the *Metanfas*, and up the River *St. Sebaftian* to *Auguftine*, had the *Metanfas* been properly guarded by the Sloops of War, or the Country Schooner ; or even by a Battery that was propofed to the South-ward of the Town, thofe Stores muft have been carried a long way over Land, and might have been intercepted by a feafonable Detachment.

When it was certain that the Gallies were not to be attacked, and the Men of War were determined to fail in a fhort Time, and carry off all their Men, Co-lonel *Vanderduffen* reprefented to them, " That he thought it would at leaft be ne-" ceffary to fend the two Men of War " Sloops into the *Metanfas* to guard that, " and either fecure the Retreat of the " Forces on *Anaftatia*, if they fhould be " reduced to one, or affift in continuing

H

" the

" the Blockade, till they should be enabled
" to act more offensively by a further Assi-
" stance." To this Proposal it was agreed,
provided the Sloops had Water enough to
get in there. And we find, that upon their
Return from Sea, a Council was held, *July*
3. wherein some of the Pilots that had
been sent to sound, declared upon Oath,
" There was not Water enough on the Bar
" of the *Metanfas* for the Sloops to go in ;
" and if they could go in, they could not
" lie safe there from a Hurricane, nor could
" they fight above one a Breast, in case
" they were attacked by the Gallies." But
the Commodore afterwards asking Mr.
Blomfield Barradel, Lieutenant of the *Wolf*
Sloop, who had been along with the Pilots, and happen'd to be a Board his Ship
that Night with some Captains, what he
had to say in that Affair, he reply'd, That
the Pilots had given their Opinion, and
that he was not then to be *examined* ; but
if they *ask'd* his Opinion, he would give
it. They then desiring he would, he
affirmed, " That there was Water enough
" on the Bar for the Sloops to get in ;
" that

" that they could lie safe from a Hurri-
" cane when in; and that there was also
" sufficient Room when in, to fight three
" a Breast, in case they were attacked."
Upon the Pilot's afterwards objecting to
their lying safe, he asked them, " Whe-
" ther they remember'd to have seen such
" an Island, when they were there?"
and when they acknowledged they did,
he replied, " that they ought to know,
" they could lie safe from a Hurricane
" under that Island." Notwithstanding
which, it was resolved afterwards in Council, that they should take off all their Men,
and sail away, leaving Captain *Townshend*
at *Frederica*.

'Tis truly surprizing that the Commodore's Assurances to the Committee of his
utmost Services in this Expedition, had
not a sufficient Influence to prevent such
a precipitate, hasty Resolution, when an
active and experienced Officer, who was
with these Pilots, contradicted them in
every Particular. Certainly such a strong
Circumstance, and the Importance, or rather Necessity of the Service might have

 very

very reasonably inclined them to a more intimate Inquiry into the true State of this Matter. But possibly the Commodore might have been allowed a Sight of those extraordinary Orders, which have been occasionally hinted at in the former Part of this Narrative.

The Commanders of the Men of War undoubtedly declared, at *Charles Town*, before their sailing on this Expedition, that they should stay no longer before the Place than the 5th of *July*. This indeed ought to have excited the Land Forces to a more vigorous Prosecution of the Enterprize ashore: Tho' it is very certain, that no Hurricane happened near so early there, in the Memory of any Inhabitant. The last, which was *August* 2. 1728, being accounted very extraordinary indeed, in Point of Time. But had they seriously apprehended so unusual a Hurricane, should it not have equally stimulated them to some notable Service, some generous Effort, before this short Term was spun out in barren Deliberations? Should it be omitted here, all others must observe, from these

frequent

frequent Confultations, without even the Confequence of an Attempt, that there was much *confulting* to *do little*; a very unufual Conduct in a *Britifh* Squadron, who commonly confult in order to Action. And if it were poffible to fuggeft any thing in Extenuation of this ftrange Irrefolution afloat, it can only be fuppofed, that as they wholly difapproved the Management on Shore, their Defpair of arriving at a general Succefs from fuch Meafures, might infect them with a greater Remiffnefs and Inattention to their diftinct Service.

Thus have I endeavoured, from fuch authentic Accounts as I have feen, to reprefent the moft obvious Errors, on all Sides, that have caufed or contributed to this Difappointment. And I can fay with fome Satisfaction on this unlucky Occafion, that I have been conducted in fuch Reprefentation by the ftricteft Attachment to Truth and Reafon, and have really endeavoured to abftract my felf from every Partiality and Prejudice whatfoever Nor can I difcern either the Honefty or Advantage

vantage of a different Conduct. I have no Hatred to any Individual concerned in this Affair, for I am too indolent to encourage any Emotion that affects me painfully; and no Favour shall oblige me to undergo the mortifying Consequences of a conscious Lye, which must be attended with the secret Contempt even of those it is intended to gratify, and must avowedly Disgust all others. I believe it would appear, upon Examination, that there is no Difference in Fact between this Narrative and a Journal of the Siege sent over by the late Captain *Norbury*, who was present at it, to the Secretary of War; only one may have been more particular than the other in different Respects and Occurrences.

What must add not a little to our Chagrin on this Occasion, is the Reflection, that tho' we are reduced to acknowledge the Enemies better Conduct, we can justly attribute little or nothing to their Courage; for excepting the Defeat at *Moosa,* where at least 300 of them surpriz'd less than half the Number of fatigu'd Men, among whom, I believe were not six

Caroli-

Carolinians) we hear of but one Person killed or wounded by them, and that by a Shot from the Gallies.   And indeed had every Man at *Moosa* behaved like Colonel *Palmer*, 'tis very possible that all the Disadvantages that little Party lay under, might have been surmounted.   It appeared upon Oath, that after he had received (in all Probability) his mortal Wound, bleeding thro' his Mouth, he kept loading his Piece, and crying " Whirra Boys, the Day is our " own, I have been in many Battles, and " never lost one."   By the same Deposition it appears, that Mr. *Hugh Mackay* cry'd out, " Every Man must shift for himself. The Colonel behaved like one determined to die or conquer ; and fell where he fixed.   Indeed his Fire was generally accounted rather extreme, and yet his Courage was so antique and unpolished, so little conversant in our senseless modern Abuses of it, that I have never heard of his engaging on any Account of his own, but like the old Heroes, his Bravery was wholly exerted on the Enemies of his Country.

Content

*Content in Times of Peace to be unknown,
And only in the Field of Battle shewn.*
ADDISON.

In short, if the Bravery of the Enemy had been truly Superior, 'tis improbable the *Carolina* Regiment could have made so regular and uninterrupted a Retreat. Our little Army undoubtedly contained many brave Men, who never had an Opportunity of exercising their Courage there, our very *Indians* telling the General, he kept on an Island to avoid fighting the *Spaniards*. And this is a convincing Circumstance that it did not require the most exquisite Conduct, the most extraordinary Vigour, to have succeeded in this Attempt. To avoid gross Mistakes, and employ that Spirit in Action, which was broke in unnecessary March and Fatigue, or evaporated in barren Deliberations must, in all human Probability, have been sufficient; especially when we observe that Mr. *Bailey,* one of the Rangers taken Prisoner at *Moosa,* affirmed, that

one

one Side of the Fort Wall was broke down and supported with Logs and Palisadoes.

Were a Man to repeat such Rumours only, as were but too much of a Piece with evident Facts, his Imagination must seem to amplify, but his Limits certainly would. It was affirmed, the first Deserter, who belonged to the General's Regiment, offered Half a Crown Sterling for a Bisket a little before. It was said, the General declared against burning and destroying the Town, saying, " What should " he do for Quarters for his People when " he had taken the Place. The like Argument would do for sparing the Castle too, since a Fort may be also necessary. The same Tenderness he was reported to extend to the very Cattle, who were to be reserved to breed from. His Name, in his own Opinion, was to produce a Surrender, the landing on *Anastatia*, which no Body disputed, was the *Conquest of Anastatia*, the coming to *Moosa* after *Palmer*'s Defeat, was the *Retaking of Moosa* --- from no Body too. But these and many other Things, however true or probable, we mention as Ru-

I

mours:

mours: It is indifferent to the main Affair if all ſhould concur to reject them.

It is undoubtedly very natural upon Miſcarriages of this kind, for Perſons to endeavour to ſhift the Diſcredit reciprocally upon one another, each endeavouring to acquit himſelf. Thus I have heard ſome Gentlemen here fond of attributing this final ill Event to not attacking the Gallies ; which I have formerly known others talk of as an inſignificant Service, which could not have availed a great deal, after the Conduct that preceded that Propoſal. The Reader may judge in this Caſe where the Merit chiefly lies, or how the Honour is to be divided. And there are not wanting Advocates on either Side. But when I hear the Conduct of the *Carolina* People arraigned on this Score, who ſeem to have been deſerted by a Friend, an Agent here, I muſt take the Liberty to ſay, I believe it very difficult to fix an Imputation of this Nature upon them. That Province was peculiarly intereſted in the Affair, they were at full 10,000 *l.* Sterling Expence by it, had voted a much larger Sum to-

wards

wards it, and would gladly have contributed still further to conclude it effectually. And as their Forces were under the
General's Command, I can't see how 'tis
possible to blame them, if they did what
they were commanded, which I never
heard even disputed. I must suppose they
were not to take the Place without proper
Commands and Directions for it : That
must have been Contempt and Mutiny.
And pray what has been done by the
Whole ? Have the *Spaniards* received a
Breach in their Fort or Fortifications, or
how many Men have they lost that we
are certain of ? While the very Horses we
had taken Prisoners were rescu'd at *Moosa*.
But if the Copy of the Report sent over
by the Province had been printed according to their Direction, their Conduct must
have remained unquestioned by every fair
Peruser. And as that Report contained
a great Number of Proofs and Papers
we are so unfortunate to want in this,
if any Fact herein asserted shall be as pub-
lickly deny'd, there is no doubt but the same
authentick Proofs may be transmitted here
again

again, if this Specimen shall not prove entiely satisfactory to all Persons.

To conclude, the ill Consequences of this Disappointment to the neighbouring Settlements would have been too obvious to particularize, even tho' they had not been already briefly enumerated : And they are render'd still less necessary by a former Remonstrance of the General Assembly of *South Carolina* to His most sacred Majesty. Nothing indeed could so effectually restore the Credit of the *British* Arms among the *Indians*, as the Reduction of that Fortress, which they consider as very difficult. The Views of *France* and *Spain* in *Europe*, seem at present to be the chief Security of those *British* Frontiers ; but if their Success at Home should give them Leisure to extend their Arms to *America* ; the particular Circumstances of *Carolina*, and very declining State of *Georgia* consider'd, it will be nearly impossible to defend and maintain those Colonies, without a large Addition of His most sacred Majesty's powerful Support and Protection.

F I N I S.